# Kap... Quest

## By
## Richard Steinitz

RICHARD STEINITZ

**KAPLAN'S QUEST**
By
Richard Steinitz
Copyright © Richard Steinitz 2014
Cover Illustration Copyright © 2014 by Novel Idea Design
Published by Enigma
(An Imprint of GMTA Publishing)

GMTA Publishing
6296 Philippi Church Rd.
Raeford, NC 28376

Printed in the U.S.A.

ISBN-13: 978-0692250372
ISBN-10: 0692250379

# DEDICATION

To my friend, editor and brother – Michael, without whose advice and assistance this book would not be what it is.

RICHARD STEINITZ

# TABLE OF CONTENTS

# Chapter I
## *Israel, 2004*

*Onkel* Samuel, as he was known in my immediate family, was an integral part of my childhood even though I never knew him, and he was presumed to have been dead for many years already (he was actually my great-uncle). I was given his name – Shmuel (Shmuel is the Hebrew version of Samuel, *Shmulik* is the diminutive nickname) and from an early age, heard stories of his athletic prowess and saw his picture prominently displayed in our house, dressed in his athletic gear. He had been a champion shot-putter in the *Maccabi HaTzai'r* (Young Maccabis) sports club in Berlin, had even taken part in the Second Maccabi Games in 1935 in Tel Aviv, and for some unfathomable reason had returned to Berlin at the end of the games.

My grandfather Ethan Kaplan, Samuel's (fraternal) twin brother, had accompanied the *Maccabi HaTzai'r* team to Palestine as a journalist, but had chosen to stay and make his home in Jerusalem, where he met my grandmother, who was also from a German-Jewish family. Their elder brother Nathan Kaplan had left Germany already in 1934, having seen the way things were going and having understood earlier than the rest of the family that it was time to get out. He had somehow managed to get an immigrant visa for Canada (though the Canadians were not very helpful about letting Jewish refugees in, to say the least), and went to live in Montreal. My great-grandparents – the parents of the three brothers – had both died in the Theresienstadt concentration camp, and we had Red Cross certificates to prove it.

The contradictory character of the *Yeckim* (as the German Jews who managed to escape the Holocaust are locally known) was well in evidence in our home. On one hand, no German-made products were ever bought (including cars), no one would ever travel to Germany unless forced to by circumstance (government service was forgivable, business dealings were frowned upon), and no chance was ever missed at bad-mouthing the German people (dead or alive) or the present German government. On the other hand, the mother tongue in my parents' house was German. Both my father and my mother were children of German immigrants, and the first language they knew and learned was German. It was only natural for them to speak German amongst themselves, especially as a way of communicating so that the children didn't understand what they were saying! We (my sister Naomi and I) learned a basic level of German at an early age, in self-defense. In our family (and I dare say in most other German immigrant households), culture was considered a German monopoly: no one composed classical music of any value except for German composers, Goethe was the greatest writer in history (far better than Shakespeare or Tolstoy) with Schiller coming in a close second, and the German countryside was the earthly reflection of the Garden of Eden.

It was an unspoken assumption in our house that I would become an athlete and so it was. I joined the local *HaPoel* sports club in our neighborhood at the age of eight and after trying various sports, decided on wrestling. Not exactly what *Onkel* Samuel had done, but close enough. My parents and grandparents came to every meet, every competition, and would shout encouragement from the side - *Oma* and *Opa* in German, my parents in Hebrew. This continued for years, through High School and up until the start of my military service. I wasn't, however, good enough to be an "Exceptional Athlete" and spend my three years wrestling for the IDF (Israel Defense Forces) team, so I went along with some of my high school friends and served in the Artillery. My wrestler's arm muscles came in very handy though, when carrying artillery shells that weighed upwards of 45 kgs each.

The army, however, has a way of changing things – for better and for worse – and by the time I had finished my three years in olive green, wrestling was no longer the focus of my life. I had decided to study History and was accepted at the Hebrew University in Jerusalem. Perhaps because of my family background, I concentrated on the period between the two World

Wars, and long before the time came for me to do a Master's Thesis, I knew exactly what it would be on.

As I said before, I never knew my *Onkel* Samuel. He had returned to Berlin after the Maccabi Games in 1935 and for a few years had corresponded with my grandfather, but with the outbreak of World War II in September 1939, this correspondence came to an end. My grandfather spent the war years working for the British Army Spokesman's Office in Jerusalem, putting his journalistic talents to use in the war effort. After the war he tried to trace his brother, and through the Red Cross, managed to find some of his old neighbors in what remained of Berlin. Their story was that Samuel had been picked up in late 1938, interrogated and released. He managed to live an almost 'normal' life for the next two years or so, but soon after the occupation of France he disappeared. From one day to the next, with no warning or visible visit by the police or Gestapo, he had simply vanished. It was assumed he had been transported to one of the concentration camps, but no trace in any of the Germans' meticulous records was ever found. It was as if he had been snatched by aliens. Through the early fifties my grandfather kept trying to find him, but soon after the Sinai campaign in 1956 he gave up – probably he just wearied of the alternating hope and pain, accepted the fact that his brother was dead and gone, and went on with his life. He never gave up telling me stories of his brother though, how much I looked like him, and how I should be an athlete in his memory. My dark, curly hair and green eyes were apparently a close match to *Onkel* Samuel's, as was my stocky build.

Years before I ever started studying history in earnest, I already dreamed of finding out what exactly happened to my *Onkel* Samuel. So when I began thinking of doing my Master's Thesis, I knew immediately what the subject would be – the last years of the Jewish community in Berlin, and specifically - the disappearance and unknown fate of my uncle. The History Department at the Mt. Scopus campus of the Hebrew University in Jerusalem has a great staff that specializes in that period, with lecturers from all over the world, including Germany, and I got to know most of them personally.

I started work on the research even before I finished my BA in European History, and spent long hours at the National Library and at the library of the *Yad V'Shem* memorial museum for the Six Million Jews that had been murdered by the Nazis, digging up what little information there was. The Pierre Gildesgame Maccabi Museum also had some material, especially on the *Maccabi HaTzai'r* organization and the Maccabi games. On a visit there, I even discovered a photograph of my uncle in the gallery and I probably needed to return to the museum to dig deeper, but it was not a priority and it would have to wait.

By the spring of 2004, I had done just about all I could in Jerusalem. My coursework was finished and I had exhausted the resources for my research that were available to me there. Despite my misgivings and instinctive revulsion at the idea, I knew it was time for me to go to Berlin. No one in the family had ever been to Germany since the war, and it was a matter of family honor never to buy any German products. I knew that my family, and especially my grandparents, would not take kindly to the idea of my traveling to that cursed country, but I knew that only there would I have any chance of finding the answers to the questions I was asking in my thesis and that I had been asking for most of my life. The family accepted my decision with great misgivings, but understood that I needed to live my own life, and do my own thing.

Two weeks before my departure, I had a surprise phone call from Montreal. Back in the early thirties, my grandfather's elder brother Nathan had emigrated to Canada. The families had kept in touch over the years, and each generation in turn had connected-up with the corresponding generation of the other branch. I had a whole bunch of Canadian cousins, of varying ages, sexes and personalities. Some I liked and some I detested, some had been to Israel on visits and some swore they would never go near it.

My second cousin Jack (Ya'akov for religious purposes) was my Canadian equivalent - more or less my age, a college athlete (fencing, of all things) and an accomplished scholar, having already finished a Master's degree in Archaeology. Our parents had encouraged us to correspond when we were young, before the days of e-mails. He had managed to understand my broken English, and we found we had many common interests, like stamps, flags of the world, and in time, girls. Up to a certain age it had been all slightly geeky, but good fun.

When he was 14, his father Daniel had taken a sabbatical from McGill University in Montreal where he taught engineering, and the whole family had spent a year in Jerusalem. There had been hope that Jack would learn Hebrew and want to come back to live in Israel, but he spent most of that year playing soccer and only on rare occasions would he visit his classroom.

We had met on several occasions after that, he had spent a whole summer in our house at the age of 17, and we got along really well. In addition to being a cousin, he was a good friend, and was the main reason I spoke English with a reasonable degree of competence. His looks, however, came from his mother's side – blond hair and green eyes. The Israeli girls just loved him! He was deep into his PhD studies, three years ahead of where I was, since he hadn't had to do army service like I had.

"Hey Sammy" he called out over the phone. "How are ya'?"

"Pretty good" I replied, "and yourself?"

"Hangin' in there." He paused and then continued: "What are you planning to do over the summer?"

"Funny you should ask," I retorted, "I'm leaving in two weeks for Berlin."

"Berlin? Why on earth would you want to go there?"

I outlined my reasons for him, including *Onkel* Samuel and the Master's thesis I was working on. When I was done, Jack said: "Coincidentally, I'm also going to Europe this summer. There's a dig I'm going to supervise in northern France, starting in July. Why don't we meet up somewhere?"

"Sounds good to me. I'll e-mail you my address and phone number in Berlin as soon as I know them, then we can decide when and where to meet. I'll probably be in need of a vacation by the time you get to France. A month and a half of digging through German archives sounds more than enough to me, 'specially since they're probably all in Gothic script - eh?"

So it was settled, we would meet in July, probably in France as he couldn't get away from the dig for too long and I would be saturated by then with old German documents. After a few pleasantries and bits of family gossip, I hung up and continued with my packing. I planned to travel light: a few changes of clothes, various jackets for the vagaries of the European climate and my laptop computer, which held everything I had amassed so far for the thesis. Admittedly this wasn't much yet, but I hoped by the time the summer was over the hard disk would be full. A copy of whatever I had so far was also on my desktop computer at home, and another copy was in my miniature office at the Hebrew University. My Masters' adviser had helped me make arrangements with the *Freie Universität* of Berlin for e-mail access, so I would be able to send messages home, and even back-up my material that way. I had also arranged with the university in Berlin for a dormitory room, which would be available to me for the entire summer, until one week before classes there started. As far as I was concerned, I was all set.

Some friends from the university were having a party that Thursday, and I went along, mainly to say goodbye. I wasn't really in a party mood, the whole idea of going to Germany had dampened my spirits in general, but I was determined to go. Many of my fellow MA students from the History Department were there as we tended to be friends with people who understood our studies. There was a nice balance between male and female students in the department, not like in the sciences or computer studies, and we often partied together. We also had a few overseas students, mainly from the US, and I had used them to improve my spoken English, since the occasional meetings with Jack were not really enough to give me a good command of the language. There had also been the odd German student from time to time, and I had offered my linguistic services to them to help them get through their courses.

I had even dated a few of my classmates, but nothing had ever developed – I was probably too involved in my studies to take dating seriously. One of the female overseas students, Yael Berkowitch, had chased me a bit more than the others, we had gone out a few times but our schedules never seemed to synch and in the end, both of us had stopped calling. Shame about that, but what can you do?

The weekend before my departure, I went to see my parents at their home in Beit HaKerem, the green and quiet quarter of Jerusalem where I grew up and they still lived, to have one good meal before I left. My mother was convinced I would starve in Berlin, that the nasty Germans would try to kill me off with bad food, and so she prepared a meal that would provide the necessary caloric intake to keep me alive for the whole summer. If I had eaten everything she put on the table, I would not have been allowed onto the plane, due to overweight.

My father took me aside after dinner and talked to me, man-to-man. He wasn't 100% at peace with the idea of me going to Berlin, but understood the personal quest that was taking me there. He himself had never been to Germany, and had no intentions of ever doing so. Spending even one penny that would somehow add to any German's wealth was, in his eyes, too much. But he didn't preach to me, and he didn't try to stop me from going, and for that I was grateful. He did, however, give me a small parcel. I asked if I could open it already, and he said: "Sure."

So I unwrapped it, and found a small Perspex picture frame, with a new copy of a photograph of the three brothers - *Onkel* Samuel, my grandfather Ethan, and Nathan the oldest brother - that hung in a prominent place in the family living room. It had been taken in 1933, just before Nathan left for Canada. My father said to me: "Keep that near you, remember who you are and where you come from."

He also gave me a slip of paper with an eight-digit number. When I looked at him quizzically, he said: "In the sixties, Germany started to pay reparations to families of Holocaust victims and people who had to flee from Germany. Oma and Opa felt they could not take the money, and neither did I. However, I convinced them to open an account in Berlin, at the Dresdener Bank, and to have their money paid into it. I don't know how much there is, I've never checked, but it should keep you in bread and cheese for a while." I thanked him for everything, he nodded back and we returned to the dinner table.

Forty-eight hours later, after a direct flight from Tel Aviv to Berlin, I was ensconced in my dormitory room close to the *Freie Universität* and ready to begin my research.

# Chapter II
## *Berlin, 2004*

The research in Berlin was hard - much harder than I had expected. Despite my reasonably fluent German (taught to me by my grandparents after Naomi and I had picked up enough to understand what we weren't supposed to, and reinforced by three years of German Language studies at university), reading documents from the thirties was excruciatingly difficult. The German bureaucrats had written most things by hand, and many of the documents were in the old Gothic script. Those I could not read well, and I often had to ask for assistance from one of the older members of the faculty in order to decipher them. Only official documents were typewritten and these provided mostly background information, nothing substantial. Letters were almost always hand-written, and I spent hours and hours deciphering these, often to find out that they were totally useless. Lists, which were part and parcel of the German character, were mainly typewritten.

On the other hand, the Nazis' penchant for documentation was a blessing for me, for it gave me a framework within which to work. I knew that if someone decided to round up the Jews in a certain district, there would be a record of it. They documented everything - from the order given, down to the contents of the suitcases taken by the deportees. There were lists of people, their home addresses, occupations, family status, dependents, property confiscated - you name it, they wrote it down. They seemed to have had a fixation with documentation, needing to keep records of everything that took place. It was weird, and sick, like everything else the Nazis did, but it made my work easier.

Using the various sources of documentation that existed in the city, I progressed fairly rapidly with the background I needed. Most of the papers were in the huge depository the American Army had established after the war, and which now had only a skeleton staff. It had been handed over to the German government in the year 2000 - the Americans had lost interest in it and the Germans tried hard to ignore its existence. I spent days in the bowels of the earth, going through miles of shelving, and rarely every seeing anyone else except for the few people employed there.

By the middle of June, I had a clear picture of Berlin in late 1938 and early 1939. The Jews that had not fled were still living there, but precariously. Their movements were controlled, they could not work and they were constantly harassed by the police and the Gestapo. Many had already been taken away under one pretext or another, but the mass deportations had not yet begun. The Final Solution was still a few years away. It would start in 1942 and only end with the Allied victory in 1945.

In the police registration records for the Charlottenburg district, I had found *Onkel* Samuel. He was living in a garret, at the top of a five story apartment house - the same house his parents had owned before it was confiscated. Like all other Jews, once a month he had to report to the police station, and every visit was recorded in the station log book. Every month, his name appeared, inscribed for posterity - *"Der Jude Samuel Kaplan"* - the Jew Samuel Kaplan. All through 1938 and 1939, his name appeared. On the 12th of each month, he would report to the desk sergeant, show his identification card and have his name entered. Next to it, he signed his name.

By the end of 1939, the signatures were growing shaky, not as firm and defiant as they had been at the beginning. Through the first half of 1940, through the *phony war* with France and then after the war began in earnest, the entries continued. In June of 1940, the Germans reached Paris and France surrendered. *Onkel* Samuel's entry for June was right on time, but that was the last one. July 12th came and went and there was no signature. This was the beginning of the real search for me: why had he stopped registering? Had he been arrested, or sent to the camps?

Just to be sure, I checked the registration records for July 10th, 11th, 13th and 14th. I thought perhaps he had signed in early or late, for some reason or other. But there was nothing. I checked the August records, too, on the off chance that he had for some reason skipped the July registration, but there was nothing there either.

I thought perhaps the police from a different district had picked him up, so I went through the records of each and every one of them, but to no avail. I searched the records of all the concentration camps I could find (and there were a lot of them), but he didn't appear anywhere. I even took on the grisly task of reading the execution records from the courts, but his name was not on any of them. It was as if, like my grandfather had said, he had been snatched by aliens.

Every piece of information, or lack thereof, I added to my data. Bit by bit, I was building up a record of the last two years before the war, and how the Jewish population of Berlin had lived (and died) during that time. I hadn't found *Onkel* Samuel, but I *was* progressing with my thesis research.

From the Charlottenburg police records, I had the address where he had lived. Fredericiastraße 38 was in a nice residential district, about 4 km from the *Zoologischer Garten Berlin* (zoo) located in the huge *Tiergarten* park, and I had walked past there frequently without taking particular notice. When I finally decided to take a look, I was pleasantly surprised. Most of Berlin had been flattened in the last days of the war, but much of this street apparently had been spared – or reconstructed with perfection. The houses looked just like they had 60 years before, with no apparent signs of mass destruction. Number 38 was in the middle of the block, typical 1900s architecture like all the others on the street, and in good condition. The entrance was locked, and as with most better buildings in old Berlin, there was a concierge who controlled who was allowed to enter. Feeling very strange, I rang the bell and spoke to the concierge through the microphone.

"Excuse me. I'm doing some research for a book, and I wanted to know if anyone in this building has lived here since before the war."

There was a longish pause, and I thought I was going to be denied entry, but then a buzzer hummed and the heavy front door clicked open. I walked into a dark and slightly musty foyer. From the right side, light shone in from an open door, and an elderly female voice called out: "*Kommen Sie rein, junger Mann.*" Come on in, young man.

She must have been at least 80, bent over like the witch from Hansel and Gretl. But the smile on her face was young and alive and she waved me into her kitchen.

"How can I help you? Would you like a cup of coffee?" This was Berliner hospitality at the grassroots level. Before I could reply, the coffee was being poured and the cake (with a heavy dose of whipped cream) was in front of me.

I decided to accept things as they appeared and go along with her approach. I drank the coffee (fair) and praised the cake (superb). She introduced herself as Frau Grenke, then asked me my name and what I wanted. I told her mine, and that I was researching a book on the neighborhood. I then gently steered the conversation around to pre-war Berlin and asked "Is there anyone living in this building now, who lived here before the war?"

Frau Grenke said: "Yes, there is", and smiled at me.

This wasn't going to be easy. I asked: "And who is that?"

She smiled again and said: "Me, of course."

Now came the critical question. "Do you remember a young man who lived here, whose name was Samuel?"

"*Aber sicher*" she said. "Of course I do. Such a nice young man, and so strong. He was an athlete."

At last, I thought, pay dirt! Just to be sure, I pulled out the picture my father had given me just before I left home, and showed it to her. "Is this the man?"

She looked at the photograph, then picked up her glasses from the kitchen table, put them on and looked again. "Yes, that's the man. His name was Samuel ... Samuel ... "

I started to speak, but she waved me to be quiet. "I know the name. Samuel Kaplinsky... no ... it was ... Kaplan. Yes, it was Kaplan, just like yours. And you look like him."

"Thank you. He was my granduncle, but I never knew him."

"Ach so," followed by a pregnant pause.

"Do you remember what became of him?"

"No. That is, I remember very well, but I don't know what became of him."

"What do you mean?"

"You know, many years ago, someone from the Red Cross came and asked me the same questions."

I had come full circle - back to the source of the little information I *did* have about *Onkel* Samuel.

I said to Frau Grenke: "Yes, I know. My grandfather had asked them to find out what became of him, but I didn't know that it was you they had talked to. Perhaps you can tell me again, you might remember something you didn't tell them then."

"I don't mind, but first another piece of cake for you, yes?"

I accepted as gratefully as I could and while she got the cake, took out my little tape-recorder so I could record what she had to say. Remembering my manners, I asked: "Do you mind if I record our conversation? That way, I don't have to write and listen at the same time."

"Please," she said, "Go right ahead."

I turned on the recorder and she then proceeded to tell me, in a nutshell, the story of my uncle's last years in Berlin. Apparently they had been friends of a sort, in addition to being neighbors. In any case, well acquainted. When he returned from Palestine in 1935, he found that there was almost no one left from the *Maccabi HaTzai'r* sports club. Most of them had gone to the Maccabi games, either as participants or as supporters, but practically none had returned. She didn't know, or perhaps didn't want to tell, why he had returned, but when he got back, he found there was no club, and that he had no job. Within weeks of his return, the family apartment had been confiscated and he moved into a little garret at the top of the house that had originally been meant for the servants. She (Frau Grenke) kept him fed when he had no money to buy food, and in general looked after him. He spent his days either working at odd jobs that people occasionally gave him, or *hanging out* with some of the few Jews that remained in Berlin.

"He would sometimes disappear for a few hours, and then return soaked in sweat. I knew he had been running through the woods outside the city, trying to stay in shape. He couldn't practice his shot-putting, but he wanted to stay in good shape, so running was the best solution." Her eyes twinkled as she remembered, and I suspected her relationship with my uncle had not been purely neighborly, despite the Nuremberg "Racial Purity Laws" that forbade intimate relations between Aryans and Jews.

Then, one day, in the autumn of 1938, he had been picked up. "I remember the *Kübelwagen* standing outside and the soldiers going up the stairs to find him. They took him away, and I was afraid I would never see him again, but late that night he returned. He didn't say anything about what had happened, and I didn't ask. It was better not to ask." She became pensive and quiet, and I debated with myself whether I could ask her more questions.

I was puzzled though, and overcame my reluctance. I asked her: "Are you sure they were soldiers? Normally the police or the Gestapo would have arrested people, especially Jews."

"It's hard to remember, but I'm pretty sure they were soldiers. I guess I didn't think too much about it at the time. But I remember the *Kübelwagen*, and it was only the army that had them - the police and the Gestapo always drove around in black Mercedes and Opels. Only the army used the *Kübelwagen*, and this one was gray – field gray, so it had to be military."

She thought for a moment, and then continued. "Life went on, and he never mentioned what had happened that day. The rest of 1938 and the first part of 1939 were more or less the same. He continued to run, and when possible, work, but the jobs became fewer and fewer and he became thinner and thinner. He wasn't really ill or anything like that, but he certainly was not in great shape. When the war started, things became much more difficult. He didn't go out much, and almost never worked. He would have starved if I hadn't fed him, but even that wasn't really enough."

I interrupted and asked: "What sort of jobs did he do? Who would hire a Jew?"

"He never really told me what he did. I just assumed it was manual labor, like taking out the rubbish or carrying boxes or things like that. The really strange thing was that several times I saw him come home and he had jumped off the back of an army truck."

Frau Grenke paused to drink some coffee, which seemed to give her strength, and then went on. "Somehow he survived, and occasionally even went out at night to run. Then came the fall of France and everyone was happy and thought the war would soon be over. I was working in a factory at the time, and would come home late. If I managed to collect some scraps of food from the lunch table, I would bring them home and give them to him to eat. One night I came home, and went up to his room to give him what passed for supper. When I opened the door, the room was empty. I thought he had gone for a run, so I left the food on the table and went back downstairs and to bed. In the morning I went upstairs again and the room was still empty and the food still on the table. They must have come for him while I was at work. I never saw him again."

We both sat still for a few minutes - she remembering and me thinking about what she had told me. None of what she had related was new, or especially revealing, but when heard first hand, it all seemed more real, and more frightening.

"Tell me Frau Grenke, was there anything in the newspapers the next day about a special round-up or anything like that?"

She shook her head. "No, nothing, but that was not unusual. Things like that were not considered newsworthy, especially with paper rationing. This was now wartime, and everything was becoming scarce."

I could see she was tiring, and had little more to add. I thanked her for her help and hospitality, and started to gather up my things, preparing to leave, when I had a thought. "Did you know any of his friends, the ones that were still in Berlin?"

She shook her head again. "There were a few, but he kept them away from here - perhaps he was afraid that someday someone would ask me about them, and what I didn't know, I couldn't tell. He was always very considerate, and worried about me a lot."

Before I left, I asked her one more question. "Frau Grenke, is there anyone else that lived in this building then, who is still alive? Do you remember the people who were living here at the time?"

She shook her head. "There might be, but I don't know anyone. There were about twenty families in the building, so that means a lot of people. People moved, or were moved, and I didn't keep track. There might be someone, somewhere, but I don't know how you could find them. I certainly don't remember any of their names."

I took my leave, but she barely noticed. Talking to me had awakened her memories, and she had drifted back 55 years in time.

When I got back to my room at the university, I logged on to the Internet and accessed the library at the Wingate Institute. I figured that there might be membership lists from *Maccabi HaTzai'r*, and if I compared them with the team lists from the Maccabi games, I might find someone who had remained in Berlin, someone who had been *Onkel* Samuel's friend. But there was nothing in the material that was available on-line, so I wrote a long letter to the librarian and sent it off by snail-mail. She knew me well from my research, and I hoped she might be able to find something.

# Chapter III
## *Berlin*

The next day, I decided to try a different approach and went back to the police records I had already gone through. I was looking for the registration of the house at Fredericiastraße 38, with the idea of getting the names of other people who had lived there in 1939. Only the Jews had had to register every month, but in Germany everyone had their address registered with the police, even today. It was a shot in the dark, but I was running out of ideas. Deep in the basement of the American archives I dug through dusty cartons and came up with something - but not much. Luck was against me this time - I found the registry book for the street, but someone had been there before me - the mice! Despite the best American technology, the rodents had found their way in, and as luck would have it, they had eaten the pages I needed! All that was left was a corner, with three names. It wasn't much, but it was all there was. I wrote them down in my notebook, and to be sure, on the laptop too.

Hans Dieter von Marburg, Brunhilde Struckmeyer and Friedrich Wilhelm Kirschhof. Three names, and nothing more, but at least it was something. The page was very chewed up and all the other information about these names, like date of birth, etc. was gone. I decided to be optimistic, and started with the current Berlin telephone directory. Who knows? Perhaps I would be lucky and find one of them living next door! But it was not to be. None of the three appeared in the phone book. That made sense, as it was more than likely that even if they had survived the war, they would most probably be dead by now. They might have left descendants, but there was no way of knowing.

Before trying to find possible descendants, I thought of another possibility. In 1950, the new Federal German government had held a census (the "national" census was actually conducted by each individual state or province) - maybe they would appear in it. If one of these three people had survived the war, there was about a 60% chance they would appear in the census. The other

21

40% would be in the archives of the DDR - the defunct German Democratic Republic in the former Soviet Zone of occupation. I assumed that the Federal census records would be in Bonn, the capital of the German Federal Republic before reunification, but a quick check on the Internet showed that they weren't. The Federal Government believes firmly in spreading national institutions around all of Germany, rather than concentrating them all in Bonn or Berlin, and the Census records were in Wiesbaden. The DDR (German Democratic Republic or East Germany) archives are preserved in the Federal Archives in Berlin-Lichterfelde, but I would leave them till later – emotionally and instinctively I felt better looking in the Federal records and I hoped I would be successful with them and not have to deal with the DDR records.

A quick check on the internet revealed that the records for 1950 were not digitized, and the only way to access them was in Wiesbaden. The internet highway had not yet reached all of Germany, so I would have to travel there and do a manual search.

# Chapter IV
## *Wiesbaden*

I had not heard anything from my cousin Jack; I had had my fill of Berlin for now, and needed a break, so the next evening I went to the *Zoologischer Garten* train station and boarded the late, overnight train for Wiesbaden. Germany is bigger than it appears, and from Berlin to Wiesbaden is about seven hours by train. When I arrived just before 8:30am, it was only a short cab ride from the train station to the National Census Archives where the census records were kept.

All the census records were on microfilm, in alphabetical order, divided by the various *Länder* or states. All I had to do was pull the reels for Berlin/1950 and start looking for the names. I was beginning to get excited - it was a bit like a game called "treasure hunt" that we used to play as kids, where you had to find various objects by deciphering clues.

I chose the names at random: first, Brunhilde Struckmeyer. I almost hoped I wouldn't find her, as her name was so extremely Germanic. I really didn't fancy interviewing some ex-Nazi camp guard. Luck was with me, I guess, as her name didn't appear. She might have died before 1950, or have moved and therefore would appear on the census roll of one of the other *Länder*, but for now I was concentrating on Berlin.

I tried Friedrich Wilhelm Kirschhof. I saw his name, and started to get excited, until I saw his age - 79! If he was 79 in 1950, that would make him ... 124 today. Not much chance of finding him alive today. He had no children or wife listed.

I held my breath as I rolled through the last reel, looking for Hans Dieter von Marburg. There were quite a few Marburgs under "M", but not the one I wanted. I made a final attempt under "v", for von Marburg, but with no success. Damn, I thought, another dead-end. I replaced the reel of micro-film in the box, and was about to return it to the shelf when I noticed that there was another reel in the box, labeled 1961.

On the principle of 'nothing ventured, nothing gained' I decided to have a look at it. Perhaps the 1950 census had missed someone? Or perhaps they had moved away during the war and returned to Berlin after the 1950 census? I loaded the 1961 reel into the viewer and began scrolling. Again, there was no record of Brunhilde, and obviously nothing for Kirschhof, and nothing under Marburg. With a sigh of resignation I spun the handles of the viewer to go to the end of the film and stopped at the v's. There were lots of 'vons', and then suddenly there he was - Hans Dieter von Marburg, single, aged 41. That made him exactly the same age as my grand-uncle would have been. Things were looking up. His current - i.e. 1961 - address was listed as Nürnbergerstrasse 27, which was just off the Kurfurstendamm – Berlin's equivalent of New York's Broadway and Paris's Champs Elysee – not far from Fredericiastraße where my uncle had lived.

I stopped and took a deep breath. I was letting myself get too excited over information that might not mean anything. 1961 was 35 years ago. Who knows where he might be now - if he was alive.

I packed up the reels of film and returned them to the archivist. As she took them, I asked: "When was the last national census?"

"1987", she replied.

"Do you have the films from then?" I asked.

"There are no films for 1987" she said, and my heart dropped. "They are all digitized, and you can search them on our computer system." At last, I thought, the modern age had reached German bureaucracy!

The thought of deciphering more official documents in German was daunting, but I had no choice. At least these were modern German, in clear computer fonts. No more handwritten Gothic script!

The computer system was fairly simple, and I had it worked out in a few minutes. I started to search for von Marburg and with a few keystrokes, I found him. I was so excited, I could barely read the entry, but there it was - Hans Dieter von Marburg! His age matched the 1950 records, and the address was given as

*Limburger Altersheim* – a retirement home about 2 kms from his previous address. I had hit pay dirt.

Then, of course, the doubts set in – what if he had died in the meantime? What if he *were* alive, but didn't remember anything? He would be 87 by now – just like Grenke and my grandfather. What if he was an old Nazi and didn't want to tell me anything? I mentally shrugged my shoulders, and packed up the box. It wouldn't help any to worry now, I'd just have to go back to Berlin and visit the *Limburger Altersheim*.

At the front desk I asked for a photocopy of the page with von Marburg's entry, paid my statutory 2.25 Euros and headed back to the train station. There was nothing to keep me in Wiesbaden. As luck would have it, there was an express train leaving for Berlin in 25 minutes, so I grabbed a quick lunch at the *Schnellinbiss* (fast-food stand) on the platform and by 9 pm I was back in my dormitory room.

# Chapter V
## *Berlin*

First thing the next morning I walked over to the *Limburger Altersheim*. The weather was fine, and I used the half hour stroll to organize my thoughts and decide what to ask von Marburg - if he was still of sound mind. The receptionist at the front desk asked me my business, and when I started to explain, she stopped me and said I would have to speak with *Herr Direktor*. The sound of the title made me think of someone from a 'thirties movie with a white coat, high collar and bowler hat, but when I was shown into his room I was pleasantly surprised. *Herr Direktor* introduced himself as Dr. Thomas Nicholas, and couldn't have been more than 40 years old, blond, blue eyed, typically Germanic looking, but with sandals on his bare feet and a tie-dyed T-shirt under his open lab coat.

I introduced myself, and told him I was doing research for my Master's, that I was looking for a former resident of Fredericiastraße 38, Herr Dieter von Marburg, in the hope that he could shed some light on the war years in that district and building, and on another resident of that building who had disappeared. I didn't go into the family relationship, just to keep things simple.

"Would it be possible to visit Herr von Marburg?" I asked. "Do you think he would be willing to answer some questions? Is he ..." I wasn't quite sure how to ask the next question.

"To answer your last question first" said Dr. Nicholas, "Herr von Marburg is lively, alert and to use an American phrase, has all his marbles. He is one of our more mentally active residents, despite his advanced years and physical handicaps, and enjoys the few visitors he has, so I don't think he would mind talking with you at all. Come, I'll take you to see him. At this time of day he is usually in the library, reading the morning papers."

I thanked Dr. Nicholas and followed him down the hall and through various corridors until we came to the library. The room was modern, with aluminum and Formica shelves and tables, fluorescent lighting and great quantities of books. Inside were a number of residents, none of whom appeared to be less than 85 years old, and all of whom were deeply engrossed in reading newspapers. Herr Direktor walked over to the end of the room and bent over to speak with a man sitting behind a table. They talked in whispers for a minute, the elderly gentleman nodding his head and then the doctor walked over to me. "Herr von Marburg would be pleased to talk with you in the reading room, in about five minutes. Is that all right with you?"

"Of course, if you'll just show me the way." I replied.

"Good, come with me and he'll meet us there." The doctor took my arm to show me out and as we left the room I saw von Marburg seem to glide out from under the table. It became clear to me that he was in a wheelchair, and then he left the library through another, wider door.

Dr. Nicholas took me to the reading room, which was in complete contrast to the library. It was dark, wood-paneled, with deep easy-chairs and leather sofas, a huge fireplace and subdued lighting from electric candles on the walls. This was a room from a previous era, if not century, something out of a gentleman's club, or some baron's castle. I had barely taken in my surroundings when the wheelchair came in, as if under its own steam. It was an electric model, controlled by a tiny joy-stick on the left armrest.

The director made the introductions and von Marburg nodded his head in the stiff, German manner I knew so well from my grandparents, extending his left arm to shake my right hand. His right shoulder ended in a folded-up empty sleeve, which explained the awkward handshake and the joystick on the chair. His lap was covered by a blanket, which fell almost to the floor and it seemed fairly obvious to me that there was little, if anything beneath it.

After the formal introductions, Dr. Nicholas excused himself and left the two of us alone. Von Marburg looked at me closely, with intelligent and friendly eyes, and then said: "Well, how can I help you, *junger Mann*?" I was getting used to being a 'young man' - first Frau Grenke, and now him.

I told him my story, as I had told it to Frau Grenke, and then added what she had told me. In addition, I explained my research methods, and how I had found his name, and traced him to the home. He nodded occasionally during my recital, and when I finished he beamed and said: "Well done, *junger Mann*. Perseverance will succeed when everything else fails. Now, what would you like to ask me?"

"First of all, do you remember your neighbor Samuel Kaplan?"

"But of course. We were good friends, and rivals." Paydirt!

"Rivals?" I asked. "In what way?"

"We were both athletes, both shot-putters, and our clubs often competed against each other. His was the Jewish sports club, and mine the university. We were neighbors, and in addition to the athletics, we often found ourselves chasing the same girls. So we were rivals, but friendly rivals, and good friends."

I could hardly believe my luck. Here was someone who knew my uncle intimately, who could tell me about his life and trials before his disappearance. But first, I had to clear up something.

"How is it that in 1949, when the Red Cross interviewed Frau Grenke, they didn't speak to you?"

He chuckled, and said: "Well, I wasn't really around to be interviewed."

When I looked at him with a question in my eyes, he went on. "I was captured at the battle of Stalingrad at the end of January 1942, and was a prisoner of the Russians until late 1954. Then they decided they had had enough of taking care of me, and shipped me back to Berlin, along with the rest of the prisoners of war that had survived their hospitality. By then, no one was looking for your uncle any more. I spent a year and a half in a rehabilitation hospital, where they tried to repair the damage that the Russians had done, but they weren't really very successful."

"Is what Frau Grenke told me an accurate picture of his life up to July 1940?"

"Yes, indeed. What she didn't tell you was that Samuel and I were in contact all through those years. When he returned from Palestine, he no longer had a sports club, and he really didn't have any other friends, and so we would often train together. When he went for those runs in the woods, it was usually with me. I would wear my university colors, and would lend him some too, so nobody took any real notice of us and we were never stopped by the police. I was busy with my studies, but we would somehow find time to train, and talk, and be together."

As he talked, he never moved his eyes from me, and then he stopped and said: "You know, you are remarkably like him. Your eyes especially - there is something that reminds me of him intensely - it is almost as if he were sitting here now." He stopped for a moment, to let the emotion pass, and I was glad of the break too. Being reminded of how similar I was to *Onkel* Samuel brought back memories and strong feelings, and I tried hard not to show how deeply I was affected.

He swallowed hard a couple of times, and cleared his throat. Clearly he too had been affected by the memories. I blew my nose, he blinked rapidly a few times, and then I pushed on. "Can you tell me anything about what happened to him? He seems to have vanished from the face of the earth, with no trace at all."

"I do not know what became of him after he disappeared, but I can fill in a few of the gaps before then. In the fall of 1938, when he was picked up, it really *was* the army that came for him. When they let him go, they told him to keep his mouth shut, but he had to talk to someone. So, on one of our runs soon thereafter, he told me what had happened."

Von Marburg was getting hoarse from all the talking, so I told him to stop while I went to look for something to drink. In the hallway I found an orderly, who directed me to a drinks machine. I brought back cups of bad coffee for both of us, and then he continued.

"The story your uncle told me was very strange. The soldiers who came for him treated him well – even politely. This by itself was unusual, to say the least. He was taken to some base in a closed truck, so he couldn't see where, and brought to the office of an Army Captain. Samuel said it was more like a job interview than an interrogation. After asking him for details of his past – school, athletics, etc., the Captain, who did not give his name or identify himself in any way, explained that he – Samuel – had been chosen to perform an important service for the Third Reich. All he would say is that from that time on, he was a protected person, that the Gestapo would not come for him and that he would be given odd jobs to keep him alive. All that he was required to do was keep in good physical shape and when the time came, he would be asked to assist the Reich in an important project. They then gave him a physical exam, took down his residential details, and brought him home."

He sipped some more coffee, grimaced, and went on. "That was all he told me, and I think it was really all he knew. He was very puzzled by the whole thing, but on the whole, seemed to have accepted it."

I asked, "That's it? He didn't say anything more at all?"

"No," said von Marburg, "Just that they had told him over and over and over again not to talk to anyone about the whole thing."

"The Captain was regular army, not SS?"

"Yes, which again was strange. The regular army did not normally have anything to do with the Jews – at least not then. Later on it was different. Oh, and he said that he thought the Captain was from an engineering unit – he had a shovel on his shoulder patch. Why an engineer should have been dealing with a so-called 'Jewish Question' is beyond me.

"And he didn't see anyone else – just that Captain and the soldiers who took him back and forth?"

"That's right. He did mention that he had seen someone he knew in the corridor, but didn't have a chance to speak to him."

"Who was that?"

"I don't know. He didn't know his name, just that he knew him from somewhere – probably from a sporting event. He didn't really have much of a social life, even before he went to Palestine. Samuel's whole life had revolved around athletics."

"And after that?" I asked.

"I have no idea. We continued to run, whenever possible, but he never mentioned the incident. Just once, after the war had begun to affect us in earnest, he said to me 'How do they expect me to stay in shape if I have nothing to eat?' It was getting harder and harder to find odd jobs, and he had little money to spend on food. Whatever jobs the mysterious Captain was supplying him with weren't enough. Even with Grenke's help, he got thinner and thinner by the day. I, too, tried to help, but my family disapproved of my friendship with Samuel and it was hard for me to smuggle food out of the house. I wasn't working either, so there was no money to spare."

"And the day he disappeared – do you know anything about it?"

"No, not a thing. By that time I had finished my studies and was on the Russian Front, freezing and trying to stay alive. I came home on leave only once, in 1942, and by that time he was long gone. To be honest, I didn't look for him very hard. I did ask Grenke about him and she told me that he was gone, and that was that. Most of my friends were gone, in one manner or another. All I did was sleep for ten days, eat whatever I could find, and pray for the war to end before I had to go back to the front. Unfortunately, my prayers were not answered. Later in 1942 I was captured by the Russians, near Stalingrad, after having lost all my toes. I spent the next 12 years in a Soviet prisoner of war camp, somewhere far beyond the Urals. And the less said about that the better."

"And you have no idea, not even a guess, what this whole thing was about?"

"*Keine Ahnung* – no idea at all. When I think about it now, it sounds very strange indeed – almost surreal. But at the time, it was just one more little facet of the whole madness that surrounded us, and I didn't give it much thought. I'm sorry I can't help you with more information."

"That's all right. You've been a great help. Is there anything I can do for you? Do you need anything?"

Von Marburg smiled. "Thank you, you're very kind, but I have all I need. The government pays the bills here, I have a distant cousin who comes once a month to visit, and the newspapers keep me occupied most of the day. What more do I need at my age?"

I packed up my papers and computer, and started to go. Before I left, I said to von Marburg: "Here's my name and phone number here in Berlin. If you think of anything else, please call me. I'll be here for a while, then I'm going to France for a few weeks and after that I'll be back here until the end of August."

31

The old man looked up at me and his eyes lit up. "Wait! There was one more thing - I remember now. The Captain asked him if he spoke French."

I made a note of this, said goodbye and left. On the way out, I stopped to thank the *Herr Direktor* for his assistance and left my name and phone number with him too. I told him to call me if von Marburg ever needed anything, and then went back to my room at the university.

The next morning I was woken up early by the phone.

"*Boker Tov*, sleepy head" came the voice from the other end.

"And the same to you, Jack" I mumbled. "I thought you had run off with a French archaeologist. At least you remember a little of your Hebrew."

"Only the important bits – greetings, personal safety and sex. How's the research going?"

"I've done a lot, but only up to a certain point. After that, it's a dead end."

"Then what you need is a break. Things are well organized here, they don't really need me at the dig all day long, so why don't you come for a visit?"

"I just got off a train 24 hours ago! However, there is nothing urgent to keep me here, so you're on. Let me wake up properly, have some coffee and check the travel arrangements and I'll call you back. By the way, where the hell are you and how do I get there?"

"I'm in Normandy – at a place on the coast called Mont St. Michel. The nearest train station with reasonable service is St. Malo – a town about 70 or 80 kms west of here. Either fly to Paris, or take a train, and then another train to St. Malo. Call me from Paris if you can, and let me know when you will get there."

"OK, I'll let you know what happens, now let me get up and have some coffee." With that, I hung up and started to get organized. A quick shower, a cup of coffee and half an hour on the internet and I was ready to call Jack back.

# Chapter VI
## *Berlin - Paris - St. Malo*

The best connection I could get was the 17:40 from Berlin to Paris, though I had to change in Frankfurt am Main. That train left Frankfurt at 22:50, and I would hopefully get a decent night's sleep then, getting into Paris early in the morning, at the Gare de l'Est. Then I had to get from the Gare de l'Est to the Gare de Montparnasse, which was not too bad a connection, especially if the Parisian cab drivers were not on strike. I would have time for a croissant and café au lait before taking the train from there to St. Malo. I had to change again in Rennes, but that wasn't too bad – just a ten minute wait, and I would get to St. Malo just before 3 P.M. All in all, it wasn't a bad trip and I preferred trains to planes in any event. It even came out a little bit cheaper than flying, though that wasn't really important, as my father's account at the Dresdener Bank in Berlin had proved to be very generous. I had no lack of funds and wouldn't have for the next few years! I called Jack back at the number he had given me, told him the plan and he agreed to pick me up from the St. Malo station the next afternoon. It wouldn't really be necessary for me to call him from Paris, but I told him I would if I had the time, just to confirm that everything was going according to plan.

I had learned to travel light in the army, so it didn't take me long to get ready. A few changes of clothes, my wash-kit and a light jacket were all I really needed, and they went into an old canvas kitbag. Last but not least, I backed up my laptop over the Internet to my computer back at the Hebrew University, and I was ready to go. The concierge was at his desk as I left the dormitory, so I told him I would be away for a week or 10 days, but that I would definitely be back. Under no circumstances was he to rent my room to anyone else! He smiled and told me not to worry, as the room was paid in advance till August 31st. The train left exactly on time. I had booked a second class coach seat, and just hoped that the train wouldn't be too crowded. Until Frankfurt it was completely full, but the overnight train to Paris was almost empty. I found an empty compartment, closed the door, pulled the blinds until the train left the station, and was pleased to find myself the only passenger in it.

I lucked out on the train. Older German railway carriages had a great system of seats – each carriage had a number of compartments, each compartment had two rows of three seats facing each other, and I was lucky enough to have a seat in one of these. The seat cushions of each can be pulled into the center of the compartment, turning the six seats effectively into three beds. As I had no fellow travelers to share the compartment with, I pulled the four seats nearest the window together, making them into a nice double bed. With the lights turned out, I slept through the entire night, waking only once when the border police came to check passports as we passed into France.

-------------------------

Paris was gray and too warm, and there were almost no cabs to be found. I had forgotten about the summer holidays which most taxi drivers took. I waited 40 minutes at the station before one arrived and agreed to take me to Montparnasse. He was rude, drove like a maniac and overcharged me, but I got to the station in time to have a Parisian breakfast, buy a guide-book about Normandy and catch my train. It was crowded with Parisians going on their summer holidays, and noisy, but I managed a quick call to Jack to say that I was on time. On the journey I read the section on Mont St. Michel, so that I wouldn't be a complete idiot when Jack started telling me about his dig, and then most of the rest of the guidebook.

My cousin picked me up at the station in a jeep that looked like it had been left behind by the American Army in 1944 – because they were ashamed to be seen riding in it! It could be heard from about half a kilometer away, and when you stood next to it, the noise was deafening. In addition, it belched black smoke like a tank laying down a smoke screen, and had only one real seat, for the driver. All the rest was *open-plan*, full of digging implements, crates and various pieces of equipment.

"If I had known that I was going to travel in style, I would have brought my tux!"

"Glad to see you too, Sammy! Please don't insult Gertrude – she gets cranky and then we'll have to walk." Jack was all smiles and dressed in tatters that once might have been jeans and a flannel shirt.

"I'm not sure that wouldn't be preferable. Where do I sit?" I wasn't sure I wanted to know the answer to that.

"Take your pick! All the seats have the same splendid view. Just be thankful the sun is shining."

"Remind me to write a letter of complaint to the management!" My canvas bag had nothing breakable in it, so I used it as a seat cushion, keeping my laptop firmly in my hands. I moved some shovels to the back and settled in on top of a wooden crate, using another as a back rest. During my army service I had traveled many miles under worse conditions, so I really had no cause to complain. Still, it was fun pulling Jack's leg and I *had* expected better transportation.

Talking was almost impossible in the open jeep, especially at the speed Jack drove, and I hung on for dear life. The countryside was beautiful, and much of the time the road was within a few meters of the sea, or to be more exact, *la Manche* - the English Channel. We sped through little Breton villages, scattering the local populace, scaring both children and livestock. Some 20 kms east of St. Malo we crossed the "border" into Normandy. Administratively, and culturally though, we were in a totally different world - Latin (i.e. French) based language and history, as opposed to Celtic (i.e. Breton). The border was, however, an arbitrary line drawn by bureaucrats, and culturally and historically, Mont St. Michel belonged to Bretagne and the Celts.

Mont Saint-Michel is a rocky tidal island, located approximately one kilometer off the country's north coast, near Avranches. The island has been a strategic point holding fortifications since ancient times, and since the 8th century AD, the location of the Saint-Michel monastery, from which it draws the name.

The tide was up as we drove over the causeway that led to the island. The causeway is a relatively recent addition – in times gone by, you could only reach the island when the tide was out. The entire island was surrounded by a wall, with one gate opening onto the causeway. Inside the gate lay a jumbled village, built on the sides of the mount, with twisted alleyways and narrow streets, one of which led up to the monastery. The village had a population of only about 50 people! The dig had taken over a small *Auberge* for its quarters and Jack had had them put another bed in his tiny room for me to sleep on. He couldn't wait to show me what they were digging up, so after a quick pit stop, I dropped my bag and laptop on the bed and we went back to the jeep for the short ride up the mount.

The monastery was even more imposing from close up than it was from across the water. If I had been a student of architecture rather than history, I think I would have changed my thesis subject on the spot! The place was amazing. I stood back from the entrance, craning my neck back so that I could take in the whole height of the edifice. Jack had to drag me inside forcibly, so entranced was I by the sight. The interior was no less impressive, but I didn't get a chance to really look at it. Jack pulled me to the side and down a corridor off the left side of the nave of the chapel, and then down about a dozen flights of spiral stairs until we came to a small landing. I was slightly out of breath by then; the descent had been both long and steep. The walls of the stairwell were made of smooth, polished limestone, which in several places seemed to be damp with dripping water, but those of the landing were totally different - still limestone, but rough and crude. On one side, there was an opening that had obviously been recently made.

"Now, let me explain what's going on," Jack said. "Have a seat on the steps while I fill you in."

I did as I was told, and he went on. "The monastery asked the University in Rennes to carry out a survey of the lower levels of the Mount, to get a full and complete picture of that part of the site. Such a survey has never been done in an orderly fashion, which means that nobody knows exactly what lies under the building that is known today as the Monastery of Mont St. Michel. The survey is a complicated business, as there are no real plans of what was built, what was destroyed over the centuries and what remains. Parts were destroyed in wars, some parts rebuilt, some collapsed due to faulty construction - you name it. Very little record was kept of the details of what remains. We know from the Monastery's primary Bible, where all events were recorded, when a certain monk or abbot decided to build a new part, but detailed records and plans are few and far between, and exactly what remains and where, is fairly murky."

He continued. "Last summer, the archaeologists from Rennes did a survey of what is today the ground floor - where we just came in - and drew up plans that show the current state of affairs. They also covered the levels just below that. I say levels, because there are no definite floors or levels like in a modern building. In one corner the stairs might go down two meters to the next level, and in another corner they might go four or five before coming to the next level. It's a real labyrinth, and no one really knows what is what, and why there are such differences. There are all sorts of dead spaces - where there is no actual room, but there should be if you go by the dimensions."

"It sounds fascinating," I said, "a bit like a haunted house where there are secret passages and hidden rooms."

"Exactly! And there certainly are lots of secret passages and hidden rooms. Again, it's not clear if they were meant to be hidden and secret, or if they just got walled up because there was no use for them anymore, or whatever. Anyway, I was given a crew of volunteers, and the North-West quadrant of the monastery to investigate. We have plans of the top level, and five flights of stairs - the first flights of the ones we just came down. After that, it's all a blank. Or it was when we started."

Jack pointed to the opening in the wall. "We did the next seven flights of stairs, but didn't go into what is on those floors – if anything. I hope we can go back to them later, if time and funds allow. Our first priority was to find out how far down the steps went. When we came down the last stairs – the twelfth flight - to where we are now, all we saw was blank walls on three sides. Obviously, or presumably, you don't build stairs unless you are going somewhere, so we assumed that there was a doorway somewhere in that blank wall, which had been sealed. We took photographs, some with infrared light and looked for differences in color and tone. We also used acoustic techniques, with a machine that works like sonar that we borrowed from the University in Rennes. The results showed us where to begin digging – in the middle of the middle wall."

He looked at his watch and went on. "Today is July 17th. We started taking the middle wall down on the 2nd of July. We did it carefully – numbering the stones in sequence, in case we ever want to put them back, and also being careful not to bring the whole Mount down on us. On the other side of the wall, the stairs continued down for about another two meters. They were similar in construction to the ones we just came down, but littered with broken bits of stone and rubble. This is where my real work began - trying to identify when the stairs were built, where they lead to, and hoping to find some artifacts from whatever period they were built in."

Jack took a deep breath, and continued. "After the first two meters, the stairs stop and there is a sloping passageway of three or four meters. Starting with the known elevation of the nave, and using a rough estimate of how far down we have gone, we guess that we were now about 2 – 3 meters below the high tide sea level. That is why you see water seeping through some of the joints between the stones on the way down."

"We used acoustics on the walls of both the stairwell and the passageway, but got nothing. That means that the stairs are probably built into the actual bedrock. We'll try again at a later date with different equipment, but that seems to be it. On the floor we found rocks and dust and little more, but nothing that can tell us anything about the history of the passageway. Basically a huge disappointment to me, and it also leaves us with the question of 'why were these stairs built?'. There was just one item that could tell us something, but I'll get back to that in a minute." He paused to take a breath, and then went on.

"Just out of curiosity, I brought along a compass one day, and took a bearing to see which way the passage was pointing – after so many steps, and twists and turns, you totally loose your sense of direction. The passage is headed at about 298 degrees, or northwest-by-west in sailor's terminology."

"At the end of the passageway was another wall - similar to the one we broke down to get in here. That by itself was curious. We took it down, just like the one at the top, and on the other side we found …"

I couldn't contain myself. "NU?" I almost shouted. "What was it? What did you find?"

Jack grinned. "Gotcha! We found … nothing. *Nada. Nichivo. Klum. Mafish.* Same thing in every language. Just a mound of earth, stone and builders' rubble blocking the passage from floor to ceiling. Under normal circumstances we would have stopped here, written a report and gone home. The report would conclude that someone, sometime long, long ago had dug the stairs for some unknown reason, and had given up for some other unknown reason."

"But …"

"Ah yes, the 'but'. Behind the second wall, when we began clearing the rubble, we found a helmet. Not a knight's helmet, not a medieval helmet, but this!" With that, he reached into his back-pack and pulled out a gray, battered helmet, no more than 50 years old. "This is what is commonly known as a 'coal scuttle'. Or in other words, a German soldier's helmet from World War II!"

"What the hell?" I exclaimed. "How did that get there? I thought this was supposed to be medieval construction."

"So did I. So did the monks. So did everyone else who had any opinion on the subject. Oh, and we also found a little notebook, about a meter or two away from the helmet. That's it – nothing else."

"When did all this happen?" I was really taken aback by this bit of news. What a weird turn of events!

"About ten days ago. I've been trying to figure it out ever since."

"And have you?"

"No, not really. I've drawn a complete blank." Jack looked at his watch and said, "It's getting late, and I'm getting hungry. Let's go back to the inn, have a wash, and go for some dinner."

"Sounds good to me. I haven't really eaten since this morning, and then all I had was a croissant and a café-au-lait."

# Chapter VII

Over dinner, we discussed the puzzle of the helmet and the notebook. Obviously, they came from the time of the German occupation, but why were they in the stairwell, and why was the stairwell walled up as if it were medieval construction? Jack said that the records from the time of the war showed that the monastery had been left alone by the occupying troops. He had gone to the town hall and read the local history, and there was no record of any troops being stationed in the monastery. The commander of the local garrison based in Avranches (just up the coast) had given clear, strict instructions to his soldiers that they were not to harass the monks, or vandalize it, but many of the soldiers would pay visits to the monastery as tourists.

"You need to find out if there is someone still alive and living here, who was here during the occupation. They might know things that aren't in the official histories."

"Good thinking, Batman!" Jack replied with a grin on his face. Reacting to my look of total bewilderment, he went on. "Never mind; a dumb, old North-American expression. But I like the idea."

"That's the difference between a historian and an archeologist," I said, teasing Jack. "We think, you dig."

I had the notebook in my hands, and began carefully paging through it. The pages were brittle from the passage of time and were very dusty from having been buried under the rubble Jack had described. The writing was almost illegible, and I really couldn't understand anything that was written there, until suddenly 'the penny dropped".

"Hey Jack" I said. "Did you try to read the notebook?"

"Yeah, but with zero success. I couldn't even recognize letters or words in the writing. It's as if it were written in some secret code or something like that."

"Well, the reason is that this is written in the old German Gothic handwriting, which basically was used by all Germans before 1941 or so. I saw this in many books and letters of my grandparents, and managed to learn a bit of it – not how to write it, but I can read it a bit. Many of the documents I've read from the archives in Berlin are written in this."

"Well, you have hidden talents, Sammy. Can you read anything in the notebook?"

"It's not easy, especially since time and dust have worked hard on the pages to make them even more indecipherable. It's going to take time to figure it all out, but it has a title page or owner's page at the beginning. The writer seems to have gone to some pains to make it look nice and readable, probably thought it was important. As far as I can tell it says: 'This notebook belongs to Captain Max von Vollendorf, of the Fifth *Pionier* Battalion of the Wehrmacht', and it gives his personnel number. The rest of the notebook, as far as I have seen so far, is not as neat and is really hard to read. It looks like this Max fellow just jotted down notes and ideas."

"Cool. That means, if anyone had the time and inclination, they could track this guy down and find out what he was doing."

"True", I said. "There are German military archives where one can do research and find things like this. Think it is worthwhile doing?"

"Well, it would help figure this out. I'm supposed to be an archaeologist, and supposed to be researching the Mount, so it would be an interesting footnote to the story."

Looking around, he caught the waiter's eye and beckoned him over. After thanking the waiter for the dinner, he asked him, in surprisingly passable, Canadian-accented French "Do you know anyone from the village who lived here during the German occupation?"

The waiter looked at him quizzically, as if to say "why on earth would you want to know?" Jack explained that he was involved in the archaeological dig in the monastery and had some questions about that time. This, too, elicited no response, and as the waiter disappeared, Jack said "Hmm. French manners, eh?"

After dinner, we left the restaurant and started climbing the Mount towards our inn. Suddenly, out of one of the little alleyways, our waiter appeared. He looked furtively left and right, then said "Try the Café de la Liberation, in St. Malo. One of the regulars there might be able to help you." Before either of us could say anything, he had ducked back into the alley and was gone.

Jack looked at me, shrugged his shoulders, and said: "Straight out of James Bond, eh?"

I could only agree. "Real cloak-and-dagger stuff. Not what I would have expected from an archaeological dig!"

We agreed that a visit to St. Malo was in order, and retired for the night.

# Chapter VIII

While Jack continued to supervise the ongoing dig, I toured the Mount as a tourist, guidebook in hand, learning as much as I could about the monastery. The place was like a maze, or a rabbit warren. Alleyways and paths, rather than streets, were the rule in the tiny town around the monastery, and in the abbey itself it wasn't much different. The various abbots over the centuries had added to the building, and some had subtracted too. Wars and the forces of nature had also contributed and taken away, and the result was a jumble of construction with little or no planning to be seen. It was obvious even to my untrained eye that there was enough here to keep an army of archaeologists busy for a long time.

When I had had enough of walking around the Mount, I worked on the notebook, trying my best to understand the chicken scratches that were this Captain's handwriting. I didn't really get very far with that.

The next evening, over *pommes-frites* and a *croque-monsieur* (french-fries and a toasted cheese sandwich), we talked about the day's events and what we were going to do next. Jack had his dig to finish – or at least this season's work, and a strange archaeological find to write up, and I should return to Berlin and my research. There was no real rush for me, but my conscience nagged me to get back to it.

Jack said: "You know, Sammy, that tunnel is really strange. Obviously there were some Germans there at some time during the war, but I can't for the life of me imagine what they would be doing there, and why. The Krauts weren't ones to waste officers and manpower on archaeological digs in the middle of a World-War."

"You're right about that." I replied. "The one person that might know about that would be this Captain Max what-ever-his-name-is."

"Well, we know that there was a garrison stationed in Avranches, which is just up the coast from here." Jack looked at his watch and thought for a minute. "My students can dig without me for a few hours tomorrow morning, why don't we go to Avranches and see what we can find?"

"We can do that, or go to St. Malo and speak to the regulars at the James Bond Cafe."

"True" said Jack, and took a coin out of his pocket. "Heads we go to St. Malo, tails to Avranches." With that, he flipped the coin in the air, caught it in one hand on the way down and slapped it onto the back of his other hand. He uncovered it and said "Avranches it is, St. Malo will have to wait."

"Fine with me," I replied, "But one of these days I'm going to have to return to Berlin."

"Another day won't kill you. We'll take Gertrude and see what we can find out."

The next morning I made Jack add some cushions and an old chair-back to the Jeep before I would agree to ride in it again. A short and windy ride took us to Avranches, where we went looking for the town library. The town looked slightly strange - both new and old at once, and we soon found out why - after four years of German occupation during the war, American air strikes had destroyed the vast majority of the town. However, it was rebuilt faithfully and many of the buildings looked genuinely 16th century, just brand new. Luckily, most of the town records had been saved, and with a little help from the librarian we found a book by a local resident, with the history of the occupation.

This time it was Jack who did the translating – my French was almost non-existent, despite several years of French lessons in high-school, and his was quite good, having grown up in bi-lingual Montreal. He ran down through the table of contents, which provided very little real information. The occupation of Avranches had been, for the most part, quiet, uneventful and almost boring, until the Normandy invasion in 1944. Then Jack stopped reading, put his finger on a page and said: "This might help."

There wasn't much – a chapter heading that read "German Army deaths during the occupation". Turning to the appropriate page, he began browsing through what was written. As he went, he just looked for any reference to a Max.

"Got it!" he announced excitedly. "It says: 'On this date, Captain Max von Vollendorf from the German occupation forces died at Mont St. Michel. His body was brought to the local garrison here in Avranches for burial.'

"This must be our man, and he's dead."

"I'm not surprised – probably something to do with that rock-fall in the tunnel."

"Could be," Jack said. "But we'll probably never know. A long time has passed since then."

"Jack" I said, "I think we've done all we can here – at least for now. I'm going to go back to Berlin tomorrow, and see if I can pick up the trail there. There must be German Army Archives from World War II somewhere, and maybe that way we can trace this Captain."

"Sounds like a plan, Sammy. But maybe you should book a train ticket before we go back to the Mont."

There was an Internet Café near the library, so I took the opportunity to check my e-mail and booked a ticket on the Internet. There is a train station in Avranches, but it is outside of town and I saw no reason not to book online. On impulse, I did an on-line search and looked up where the German Army archives were, and found that they were not in Berlin as I had thought! They were located in the small city of Freiburg, in the south of Germany, just by the Black Forest.

I told Jack and quickly canceled my booking to Berlin. Freiburg was really not on the direct route back there, but I figured it would be easier to go there now, rather than return to Berlin and then make another trip.

Getting to Freiburg by train was possible, but it involved seven changes! St. Malo, then Rennes, Paris Montparnasse, Paris Metro, Paris Est, Kehl, Orteneau, Offenburg, Freiburg! Some of the changes were only minutes apart, so I would have to pray hard that none of the trains were delayed, and that I would find my way on the various platforms.

The Deutsche Bahn (German Railway) site gave me clear directions, including where to change and how to transfer from one Paris station to another. It even told you at which Metro station to get on and off, the number of the train and which stairs to use! German efficiency was frightening, as always.

So I booked the trip for the following day, using my credit card, and we went back to the Mont to eat and pack. Dinner was *pommes-frites* (French Fries) and a *saucisse* (sausage), with a glass of local wine. We stayed late in the cafe, just talking about things like family and history.

The next day Jack took me to the St. Malo train station in Gertrude, arriving just in time for my train at 12:50. "Take care, Sammy. It was great seeing you here, and I can't wait to hear what you come up with from the archives."

"Don't worry Jack, I'll be in touch as soon as I learn anything. When do you finish the dig here?"

"I have to be here another 10 days or so, and then I should to go back to school. I'm supposed to be teaching a class starting Sept. 6th. However, I have a couple of weeks that are basically free, so if you need me, let me know before I leave."

"Fine. I'll be in touch. Speak to you soon." With that, I got on the train, found my seat and settled in. Seven changes and 10 hours later, I was in Freiburg.

# Chapter IX
## *Freiburg*

I got to Freiburg on time – no surprise there. It was 11pm in a town I didn't know, I was tired and didn't feel up to studying a map. I had checked before getting on the train in St. Malo, and knew that there was a youth hostel in the city. The easiest thing was to take a taxi, and I found one standing alone outside the station entrance.

"*Jugendherberge Freiburg, Kartäuserstrasse 151, bitte.*" I told the driver.

It was almost midnight by the time I got to the hostel and it was closed and locked up like a maximum security prison. Youth Hostel Association rules state that hostels should be closed at 11pm, and in super-law-abiding Germany there was little chance they would break this rule. Luckily for me, the night manager was still awake, and heard me banging on the front door. A few words of explanation and a bit of pleading got him to let me in, and sign the register, noting the time as 22:59 – one minute before closing time! My suspicions were aroused by his readiness to break the rules, and he indeed turned out to be not a local, but a visitor from New Zealand.

There was no chance of oversleeping in this place. At 7AM, bugle calls were broadcast over the public address system – in every single room. Breakfast was from 7:30 to 8:15, and by 8:16 the tables were cleared and the dining room was empty. I hurried to grab my bags and sign out, as the hostel closed at 9AM – God forbid someone might stay in their room during the day.

On my way out, I stopped at the reception desk and asked the friendly Kiwi if he knew how to get to the Military Archives. He did, and even called me a cab so that I could get there with no problem. He was a nice change from the German staff and attitudes.

The *Bundesarchiv – Militärarchiv* was open and ready for business by the time I got there. I told the receptionist that I was a researcher from the Freie Universität of Berlin and produced my faculty card from there – I figured I would get better cooperation that way, than if I gave her my Israeli credentials. Just to be sure, I told her I was looking for the records of a distant family member. She was cooperative and friendly, and showed me the room where personnel records were kept.

The primary search of the micro fiche personnel files didn't take long and produced details of the Captain immediately, with the date of his death and location according to what we already knew, though the location was listed as Avranches, and not Mont St. Michel. What I wanted to find was additional information – place of birth, family, etc. There was little there, just year of birth (1885) and place of birth (Vollendorf, Ostpreussen, or East Prussia). Father was listed as Walter Vollendorf, mother as Irmegard Schultz, both also born in Vollendorf. Strangely, neither parent's name was listed with the noble 'von', though the Captain's was. And he had a wife – one Ingrid Schmiltz.

The information was good to have, but it didn't really help very much. I really wanted to know what the Captain had been doing on the Mont, and why. On a hunch, I asked for the non-micro fiche record and was early enough to have my request included in the morning batch. The Captain's file was thin and the papers inside were brown, faded and brittle. One sheet was the record of his induction into the army, and included a photograph. At last I had a picture of whom I was looking for! The induction record also recorded the fact that he was immediately given the rank of Captain – a strange fact, given the German Army's record for strict adherence to regulations. Why would someone be inducted into the army with the immediate rank of Captain? This seemed to me to smell slightly – something was not quite *kosher.* Before returning the file, I looked at the rest of the papers. One was a result of his physical examination, showing him to be severely near-sighted, short (only 1 meter 55 cm) and overweight at 87 kilograms. Curiouser and curiouser! Certainly not the image of the Aryan soldier one would expect from an 'instant Captain'.

Another sheet was a letter of recommendation from the Department of Medieval History at Göttingen University, stating that Prof. Max von Vollendorf was a member of the faculty, had been so for 8 years, and listed his published papers. Again, not a normal record for an Army Captain.

The last page was the strangest. It was a typed recommendation, or perhaps order would be a better description, 'suggesting' that Prof. Max von Vollendorf be immediately inducted into the Wehrmacht with the rank of *Hauptmann* (Captain). It was signed by no-less than Rudolph Hess, Hitler's deputy in the party and a minister in the government. Why would Hess be involved with an obscure university professor's induction into the Wehrmacht? Was he a relative? A friend? Hess would become famous later during the war for his flight to England in 1941, on an attempted peace-mission, but this obviously had nothing to do with the little captain. I noticed that the date on this recommendation was 1942, but that must have been a 'typo', as Hess had flown to England already in 1941.

I filled out a form for photocopies and a CD-Rom copy of all the pages in the file, handed it in and paid cash for them. Since it might take weeks before I received them, I had made copious notes on my laptop. The whole file was a mystery to me, and made little sense. Further research was needed, and there were two obvious things to do. One was to go to Göttingen University, where von Vollendorf had been a professor, and the other was to try and find any relatives of his that might still be living. As the town of Vollendorf was now part of Poland, there was little point in going there – the chances of any Germans still living there were next to nil. So it was either back to the National Archives in Wiesbaden to try and find relatives, or a visit to the little university town of Göttingen. The direct route back to Berlin went through neither place, and family was probably more important than the university, so another visit to Wiesbaden seemed to be the answer.

I was getting a bit tired of traveling, and was really looking forward to getting back to my room in Berlin, but it made more sense to go to Wiesbaden now, rather than return at a later date. I returned to the Youth Hostel, packed my bag and the friendly New Zealander checked the train schedules for me. I managed to catch the 15:40 InterCity Express and we got into Wiesbaden at 17:32, where I took a cab to the youth hostel. It wasn't as nice as the one in Freiburg, but it was OK. Clean sheets and a clean shower were all I wanted, and that was a 99.99% guarantee at any German hostel.

The next morning, the lady at the archives remembered me and gave me a seat at one of the computer terminals, since I thought that only the latest census would be of any help – that of 1987. I started to look through the files of the various *Länder* – the so-called 'national census' was a compilation of the census' of the *Länder*. There were a fair number of Vollendorfs, and this meant that I had to check each and everyone for family histories and birthplaces. There were lots of Vollendorfs, but not a single "von Vollendorf". I assumed this was some fluke of bureaucracy, that some clerk had decided he didn't like the ex-nobility and had removed the 'von' from all the names. In addition, only those that had any family connection to the town of Vollendorf in East Prussia were of any interest. As the Captain was born in 1885, it seemed highly unlikely that any brothers or sisters he might have had would be alive today, but if I could find children of any siblings, there was a chance that they might know something about the Captain. It was slow work, checking the files, and not 100% successful, as not all the respondents had listed their uncles and aunts on the forms. I did manage to find two possibilities – a Wilhelm Vollendorf and a Frieda Volker (née Vollendorf), who were born in 1881 and 1890. Both were deceased, but they were listed on the form filled out by a Henning Vollendorf who had listed them as his father and aunt. Henning Vollendorf was born in 1914, which would make him 90 today, if he were still alive. As luck had it, his address was listed in Berlin, which meant I could go back there. I paid for a copy of the records and headed for the train station. There was an 11:30 train, and I just managed to get to the station in time to buy a ticket and find a seat. By 5pm I was back in my dorm room, totally exhausted from my travels and searches – all I wanted to do was sleep! After a quick shower and before crawling into bed, I sent a short email to Jack in Mont St. Michel to up-date him on the results of my searches.

# Chapter X
## *Berlin*

I took a day to arrange my notes from the trip, answer emails that had backed-up, and do some chores. I also caught up on lost sleep – all this traveling had taken its toll on me.

The next morning I checked the Berlin phone book for an address for Henning Vollendorf, but there was none. I feared that this was the end of the story, that he was dead, and that I would never figure out what had taken place so many years ago. There was one last hope – that he was alive, but living in an old-age home. There were a large number of such institutions in Berlin, to say nothing of the rest of Germany, but I had to start somewhere. Rather than go through the Berlin Yellow Pages and visit all the old-age homes listed there, I decided to go and see Hans Dieter von Marburg. I owed him a visit, to bring him up to date on my research, and perhaps someone at the *Limburger Altersheim* would have an idea how to find Vollendorf.

At the Altersheim I was greeted like a long-lost son. Anyone that came to visit was greeted warmly, but it seems that von Marburg had told his and my stories to everyone that would listen. Dr. Nicholas - *Herr Direktor* to the residents and staff – came out to see me and took me aside for a short chat.

"Herr von Marburg is doing well, and I'm sure he will be very happy to see you. Have you made any progress in your search?" The doctor was fascinated with the whole story and wanted to know what the outcome was. I told him that I thought it was only proper that I tell von Marburg first, and after seeing him, I would come to speak with the doctor again.

"Of course" he replied, "That is the way it should be. It's nice to see that you have such proper manners – they are so rare these days." He escorted me down to the reading room, where the old man was just as I had left him the last time – sitting by the fire, reading his newspaper.

Hans Dieter von Marburg looked up from his reading, saw me standing there and a huge smile came over his face. "Ach, *junger Mann*" he said. "You've come back to see me again, and by the smile on your face, I assume that you have had some success in your searches. Come sit down next to me and tell me what you have discovered."

When I reached the end of my tale, von Marburg sighed and said to me: "What a strange story. I wish I could help you progress further with this, but I'm afraid I have no more information. I do not know the name von Vollendorf and I had no contact with *Pionier* Battalions in the war. I think I was once in the town of Vollendorf, during the war, but I don't remember anything about it. Perhaps Herr Direktor can help you with locating this man."

I promised him that I would keep him informed, and that I would bring better coffee next time, and left him to his newspaper. On the way out, I stopped by at Herr Direktor's office and gave him a shortened version of what had transpired since I last saw him. On the off chance that he might be able to help, I told him about my search for Henning Vollendorf.

"I don't know the man, or the name, but I do have colleagues in some of the other old-age homes here in Berlin. Let me make a few phone calls and see if anyone knows anything. I have a half-hour free right now, so if you want to go back to Herr von Marburg and chat for a while, I'll let you know when I'm done."

I thanked him profusely, as this was really above and beyond his normal duties, and I took the opportunity to go out and visit the coffeehouse down the street. A short walk, a few minutes of explanations and requests, and I was back at the Altersheim, with three cardboard cups of the best Berliner Kaffee, with mounds of Schlag (whipped cream). I left one on Dr. Thomas's desk and took the other two to the library, where I found von Marburg dozing in his chair. Before I could even open my mouth, he awoke with a huge smile on his face, and said *"Echter Berliner Kaffee!* How wonderful. And how kind of you, *junger Mann!"*

Dr. Nicholas came in about ten minutes later, with a smile on his face. "This is your lucky day Herr Kaplan!"

I looked up at him from my easy chair and said, "You're joking! You mean you've found Henning Vollendorf?"

"Yes indeed! I made a few phone calls to my colleagues and on the third attempt, I hit the bull's eye! The *Pflegeheim* [convalescent home] *Marienstrasse* has a resident named Henning Vollendorf. I can't guarantee that this is the same person that you are looking for, but the chances are pretty good I would imagine."

I was taken aback at my amazing luck, but had enough presence of mind to ask Dr. Nicholas for the address of the Pflegeheim. He pulled his prescription pad out of his back jeans pocket, tore off a page and wrote the address down on it. "Good luck with your search, and please keep us informed of your progress." Von Marburg nodded his head in vigorous agreement and promised to stay in touch. I left them deep in conversation, and headed out towards Marienstrasse – I was too psyched to leave this to another day.

I hailed a taxi and gave him the address on Marienstrasse – this was no day to save on cab fares. At the *Pflegeheim Marienstrasse* I went to the reception, and asked to speak with the director. A few minutes later he appeared – a stern looking man of about 60, dressed in white lab-coat and rimless spectacles, with a little goatee – somewhat like a middle-aged version of Sigmund Freud. I introduced myself and gave him the shortened version of my story and explained why I wanted to speak with Henning Vollendorf.

He nodded his head several times during my explanation and then said "I understand. I spoke with Herr Direktor Thomas when he called and he gave me the same story. It is indeed a strange tale, and I'm sure that Herr Vollendorf will be interested in it too. I'll have an orderly bring him to the library, so please follow me."

Henning Vollendorf arrived in a wheelchair, pushed by an orderly. He was obviously not in the best of health, but smiled when Herr Direktor introduced me. He nodded at me, and said in a soft voice, "Please tell me your story *junger Mann*, I would be very interested in hearing it."

I started out by making sure I had the right man. "Are you the son of Wilhelm Vollendorf, and the first cousin of Max von Vollendorf, son of Walter and Irmegard Vollendorf?"

He nodded in agreement. Then, once again, I told the story from beginning to end, and Vollendorf listened intensely, frowning deeply when the name of Max von Vollendorf was mentioned. When I was done, he said to me: "Fascinating - and how can I help you?"

"Well" I said, "I have a number of questions about Max von Vollendorf, which I hope you can answer."

"First of all" said Henning in a tone of annoyance, "His true name was Max Vollendorf. There never was any nobility in our family, and no one ever used the name "von Vollendorf" except for him. He had no right to use the 'von' but in those days it was useful to him and no one ever checked on him I guess."

"I understand. That clears up some things already. Can you tell me anything about him? Did you know him well? Do you know anything about his family? His wife? Did he have children?"

"*Langsam, langsam junger Mann!*" He chuckled softly and continued. "Not so fast."

"I'm sorry Herr Vollendorf, I get excited easily."

"At my age, that's not a good idea." He nodded again, and went on: "Max was a nasty fellow from an early age, and I had as little to do with him as possible. So did most of the family. He was not very ... shall we say... masculine? This did not fit well with our family, which, though not of the nobility, was a very old and respectable family. As for his wife, Ingrid, well – she was nasty too, but in a different way, and really hated Max. He only married her due to pressure from his parents, and to try and fit in to regular society. I guess she discovered his true character only after they got married and in those days, once you were married, then in general it was too late to do anything about it. So she spent most of her time making his life as miserable as possible."

"Were there any other family members who might know more?" I asked.

Henning Vollendorf replied, "They had no children, thank God, and he was an only child. She had a brother actually, I remember now, he was a high officer in the Wehrmacht – perhaps even a General. But I don't know anything more about him."

I looked at my notes from the *Militärarchiv* and said to him: "Her name was Ingrid Schmiltz, so I guess this General's name would be Schmiltz too. Maybe I can find some of his family."

Vollendorf was getting tired, but asked me "Why are you looking for the family?"

"I'm trying to find out what Max was doing in Mont-Saint-Michel, and maybe there are some papers, perhaps with the family, that can help me figure this out. Perhaps this General had something to do with Max joining the Wehrmacht straight-away as a Captain."

"Good luck, *junger Mann*. I cannot think of any reason he would join the Wehrmacht at all, he was about the most unsuitable person I can think of to be a soldier. If I had ever thought of him as a soldier – which I didn't – I would have imagined him a simple infantryman, and probably dead somewhere on the Russian steppes. I hope you find what you are looking for, but if it had anything to do with Max, I doubt that it will be good."

"One last question, if you don't mind." He nodded. "You had an aunt – Frieda Volker. Did she have any children?"

He took a minute before answering. "I have not heard of, nor thought about, my aunt Frieda in about sixty years or more. She and her husband Alfred left Germany in the early 1930s, and the family cut off all connections with her. I have no idea what became of her, where she went, or if she had any family. I don't even know if she is alive or dead, though she would be over a hundred by now, so the chances of her being alive are pretty slim."

I took some quick notes, thanked Henning Vollendorf, and left the room. On my way out I stopped in to say thank you to Herr Direktor and went back to my room.

# Chapter XI

I went back to my dormitory and thought about my next move. A call from Jack interrupted my thoughts: "What's new in Berlin?" he shouted from the other end of the line.

"Jack, the phone works great, you don't have to shout." I told him. "I'm crawling forward with this business, when I want to run! It's really frustrating – every little bit of information brings a whole new line of inquiry, and I don't feel like I'm making any real progress." I then proceeded to tell him of my visit with Henning Vollendorf.

"Doesn't sound like you got much out of him." he said.

"No, not really. The only thing new is this general – Max's brother-in-law. I hate to say it, but I think I'll have to go back to the *Militärarchiv* in Freiburg again. Another train trip – at this rate, I should be getting frequent flyer points on the *Deutsche Bahn*! And I'm getting bum-blisters."

"Can't you fly" Jack asked?

"Spoken like a true Canadian." I answered. "Not every city in Germany has an airport. The nearest one to Freiburg would be Basel, and then I would have to take a train anyhow to get to Freiburg – and cross the Swiss-German border."

"Bummer" he replied. "Wish I could help you but I'm stuck here for another week at least."

"Thanks for the offer, Jack. I'll let you know how I get on and if I'm still sane in another week, I'll call you for reinforcements."

I hung up and went back online to check the train schedules. I needed another day or two to catch up, do my laundry and in general get my life a bit better organized. The next morning, after a late breakfast, I headed for the *Schneeweiss* laundry down the street. The girl behind the counter giggled at my mixed pile of whites and colors (something no good German would ever dare to do) and promised to have them ready the next morning at 10. Next stop was the SPAR mini-market, for some basics – milk, bread, cheese and vegetables – the staples of my Israeli breakfasts and dinners. Just to make me feel at home, I got some orange juice and saw that it was a product of Kibbutz Givat Haim. Part of Israel's revenge on Germany was its citrus crop!

If I got up early enough on the day after tomorrow, I could catch an Intercity Express train at 8:30 in the morning, and be in Freiburg by 3 o'clock in the afternoon. It would cost more than a regular train, but if I was lucky and found what I was looking for at the military archives quickly, before they closed for the evening, I could then take a slow train back over night. There was a 10pm train that got to Berlin at 7:20 in the morning, and I might just treat myself to a sleeping car, rather than hope for an empty seat compartment. I hadn't spent very much of the money that had accrued in my and grandfather's account in Berlin, so I didn't feel guilty about this minor luxury. I needed to learn how to spend the money I had in the account, but it was difficult – it totally went against my upbringing.

I packed the bare necessities I would need, went down to the corner *pinte* to have a quick sausage and a beer, and turned in early after setting my alarm for 6:30.

# Chapter XII

I picked up my laundry at 10 – folded, ironed and starched, including the underwear – and took it all back to my room. I had almost an entire day free, something I wasn't used to, and took the opportunity to do some sightseeing in Berlin. The city was fascinating, being rebuilt at an enormous pace, but I couldn't get into the mood for being a tourist in this city. There was just too much history, too many family memories and stories, to be able to really enjoy myself. Though there were many Israelis now living in Berlin, and many Jewish immigrants from the former Soviet Union, I could not imagine myself living there. Some things just were not meant to be.

The next morning the train left at 8 and I just made it. I splurged on a dining car breakfast, slept for a few hours and then had a real lunch in the dining car. White linen table cloths and fine china made a nice change from the fast food I had been living on. There was no real reason for me to be living so frugally, I had plenty of money in the bank, but I guess it was old habits that had been ingrained in me since childhood. Growing up in Israel there had never been an excess of money, and the family ethos had been very strong on "don't waste money". I justified my 'waste' by remembering where the money had come from and what it was supposed to be atoning for.

At 3:00 pm sharp the train pulled in to Freiburg, and I took a cab to the *Militärarchiv*. The receptionist actually remembered me and helped me find the file I was looking for. There was only one General Schmiltz in the files – thank God – and I quickly extracted the information I needed. Generalmajor Wilhelm Siegesmund Schmiltz, born in Göttingen 1880, missing in action on the Russian Front, presumed dead, March 15th, 1942. Married to Ilse Margarete Steinpiltz, children Fritz Georg (b. 1923) and Liesl Beatrix (b. 1930).

Out of curiosity, and because he would have been exactly the right age to have served in the German Army during the war, I check the *Militärarchiv* to see if there was any record for Fritz Georg Schmiltz. I found his file with ease – the birth date and the parents names were a perfect match to the General's records. Born 1923, missing from his unit in France 1942. That was a curious phrase, as it didn't say missing in action. When I turned the page, I found another sheet of paper, issued by a Military Court! My knowledge of German legal terminology was limited to say the least, but it seemed to be an arrest order for Fritz Schmiltz, having been found guilty in absentia on the charge of Desertion in the Face of the Enemy!

Wow, I thought. That can't have helped his father's career. Then I checked the date - he had gone missing on March 30th – two weeks after his father's presumed death on the Russian Front. I wondered if there was a cause and effect here, but as it wasn't directly connected to the Mont St. Michel business, I just wrote some notes and left it at that.

My job here in Freiburg was done, but I hesitated before heading back towards the train station. I needed to check with the census, to see if Liesl Beatrix Schmiltz were still alive, and if not, whether I could trace any descendants she might have had. Looking at a map of Germany, it made little sense for me to return to Berlin. I would go to Wiesbaden to check the census records. If I had a little bit of luck, any Schmiltz descendants would be in or around their home town of Göttingen, which made a more or less direct line: Freiburg-Wiesbaden-Göttingen and then (hopefully) back to Berlin. I had had the foresight to pick up a copy of the massive *Deutsche Bahn* time table when I left Berlin, and I could now check my options on the run. It was now 16:30 pm – if I ran (literally), I might just make the 16:56 train which would get me to Wiesbaden at 18:06. If I missed that, then there was another train 17:49, getting me to Wiesbaden at 20:54 – still a reasonable hour to find a place to sleep.

I missed the 16:56 train, but that gave me time to have a bite to eat and try to call Jack. I had a 20 Euro *Telefonkarte* with enough credit still on to chat for quite a while. There was a bright yellow old-type phone-booth just by the snack bar, and the door was sufficiently well insulated so that I could actually hear Jack on the other end – despite the trains coming and going.

"Hiya Cousin" I said.

"Hey Sammy! How's the detective business going?"

"I've made a little bit of progress," I replied. I brought him up to speed on the latest developments and gave him my proposed schedule – Wiesbaden tomorrow, then probably Göttingen. "How's the dig going? Any progress? Any new finds?"

"Actually, the dig is almost done for the summer, though there is still a lot of work to be done. Looks like I'll be back again next year.

"Great! Any chance of you joining me here or in Göttingen?

"Maybe in a day or two – call me when you are done with the census people and I'll see how the situation is here. By the way, the Captain's notebook is still with me. You'll probably have more use for it than I will, so perhaps I'll just send it to you by registered mail."

"Thanks, Jack. I hope you can meet me here and bring it along, because the thought of losing that in the mail is bit too much – only as a last resort I'd ask you to mail it. I don't trust postal services, and especially not the French!"

"Understood, Sammy. I'll wait for your call. Good luck!"

# Chapter XIII

Wiesbaden was grim and rainy, which suited my mood. I was tired and fairly fed up with running around this country searching for traces of nasty people. I really needed a good night's sleep and some encouragement. There was only one cab outside the train station when I arrived, and thankfully the driver was in it and awake. I asked him to take me to the best hotel he knew and he jumped at the chance – I don't think he had really expected to get a fare at this time of night. It was a short ride to the Radisson Blu Schwarzer Bock, and the receptionist was efficient and friendly. Ten minutes later I was in my room and heading for a hot shower.

Since I was being decadent anyhow, I decided to order room service, and a late wake-up call for the morning. An outrageously expensive sandwich and a local König Ludwig Dunkel beer put me in a better mood. I turned the air conditioning up high, pulled the blanket up to my ears and was asleep in a flash.

The phone rang at 8:30 AM, I picked it up in my sleep and heard a recorded voice in German telling me it was time to get up – or else! I treated myself to another shower (there's nothing like a hotel shower as far as water pressure and temperature are concerned) and after a quick breakfast headed out again – in the rain.

The census bureau people were busy and I had to wait for half an hour before anyone would talk to me. Finally, I was taken to a little cubicle with a micro-film reader, and the clerk brought me the reels for the last two censuses for the State of Niedersachsen (Lower Saxony), which includes Göttingen.

I started by looking for General Schmiltz' son Fritz – on the off chance that he might have escaped German Army justice and be still alive and living in Germany. I didn't find him, so I tried the daughter - Liesl Beatrix, not really believing I'd succeed. But my luck had changed, and there she was, in the latest census, and living near Göttingen. Liesl Beatrix Schmiltz, a.k.a. Sister Beate Schmiltz, daughter of Generalmajor Wilhelm Siegesmund Schmiltz and Ilse Margarete Schmiltz (née Steinpiltz). Her place of employment was listed as the Göttingen University Hospital, and her address was in the town of Nikolausberg. I had hit pay dirt! She should be about 74 now, passed the age of retirement, but apparently still working, so she should be able to give me some information. I printed out a complete copy of her record, paid for the print and left.

There was nothing more for me to do in Wiesbaden, so I headed for the train-station. Once there, I checked the schedule (I had half an hour till the next train to Göttingen) and then called Jack.

"You're in luck" he answered. "I'm done here now for the season, all the students have been sent home, the tunnel has been sealed, and I'm a free man."

"Great! So find your way to the train station and start making your way towards Göttingen. I'll be there in a few hours, and will be staying at the youth hostel. Leave me a message at the reception, telling me when you are going to arrive and I'll meet your train. I have the information we need, and the address, so I'll wait for you to arrive before I speak with the General's daughter, Sister Beate."

"Sounds good to me" Jack replied, and hung up. I found the platform for the Göttingen train, and got there in time to board and find my seat before the train left.

# Chapter XIV

The trip took only about two and a half hours, including a quick change in Frankfurt, and I was at the youth hostel by late afternoon. The receptionist booked me in, and I asked for a bed for Jack too, even though I had no idea when he would arrive. This was a modern hostel, and had small rooms for two or four people, in addition to the classic dormitory style rooms, so I took a double room for the two of us. It was slightly more expensive, but still dirt-cheap compared to a proper hotel. As I had nothing better to do, I took the time to walk around the city and get oriented, and see where the University Hospital was in relation to our hostel. Göttingen is a university town, with lots of old half-timbered houses and little more, at least not in the center. It seemed pretty and pleasant, a bit like many other university towns, but it didn't have the campus buildings in the town.

After a quick bite to eat in the center of town, I got back to the hostel around 9pm, to find a message from Jack. His train would get in at 8:47 AM, which was perfect. I hoped he would get some sleep on the train, as I planned on picking him up and going straight to the hospital to try and find Sister Beate. It might not be the nicest way of approaching her, but I didn't want to call her and have her slam the phone down on me. I had been lucky so far in my searches, everyone had been friendly and helpful, but I didn't want to push my luck!

The statutory morning bugle went off at 7am, piped into all the rooms through a (very) loudspeaker system. God forbid anyone should sleep past the official wake-up time! Despite their history and everything associated with it, the Germans seemed to be unable to shake their military past completely. I didn't really mind about the wake-up call, as I had to meet Jack's train, but the method could have been a bit gentler. Oh well …

A quick slice of bread and jam, a cup of coffee and I was out of there. I told the receptionist that I would be back in the evening with Jack, and he was quick to inform me that I would be charged for his bed last night, even though he had not slept in it. I assured him that was fine, I would not argue about it and that we would pay for both nights the next morning. His look said "I don't trust these foreigners, they'll probably run away early in the morning to avoid paying" but he didn't say a word, just made a note in the guest-book.

"How was the trip?" I inquired when Jack alighted from his train.

"Fine" said Jack, "and I managed to sleep most of the way. Do you have any further news or information?"

"No," I replied. "I figured it was best just to start from the very beginning with this woman and hope for the best."

We walked out of the station and took a cab from the rank, telling him to go to the University Hospital. Being a well informed cab-driver, he asked: "Which part? The hospital is located in many different buildings."

Not knowing where we wanted to go, I said "Just take us to the administration building, please." It was a short ride, we could easily have walked it, if we had known where we were going!

At the information desk in the administration building, I asked where I could find Sister Beate Schmiltz. The receptionist said "She works in the hospice, next to the Oncology Department. That's in the next building – go out the door, turn left, and on the fourth floor."

I thanked her and we left. In the elevator in the next building, the Hospice was clearly listed on the fourth floor, left wing. There were times when I simply adored German efficiency! At the entrance to the Hospice, there was another reception desk, but this time when I asked for Sister Beate Schmiltz, the nurse behind the desk asked me why I wanted to see her? I told her that it was a personal matter, concerning her family, that no, she did not know me but I hoped that she would be able to find time to speak with me. She looked at me as if I was trying to steal the crown jewels, but picked up the phone and spoke rapid, colloquial German into the receiver. I could barely understand more than 50% of what she said – her local accent was so thick!

The receptionist hung up, and said to me: "Sister Beate will be able to see you for a few minutes in about a quarter of an hour. Sit over in the corner and wait for her there." I was scared to say anything back to her so I just nodded in acquiescence and pulled

Jack over to a pair of overstuffed armchairs. I gave him a quick review of what had transpired, and then we waited.

A quarter of an hour later (almost to the second), a diminutive nurse/nun came out through the double-doors behind the receptionist and asked who wanted to speak with her. The receptionist pointed in our direction and she came over. She could not have been more than one meter fifty, at the most, and had pure white hair sticking out from under her nurses' cap (or was it a nun's wimple? It was hard to tell.)

I motioned to Jack to get her a chair, and introduced myself and Jack. Just to be 100% sure, I asked her if she was indeed the daughter of Generalmajor Wilhelm Siegesmund Schmiltz and Ilse Margarete Schmiltz (née Steinplitz). She nodded but said nothing and I asked her to please sit down. I gave her a very condensed version of my story, and at the end said: "The reason we have come to see you is to find out if by any chance you have any papers that belonged to your Uncle Max Vollendorf. I am hoping that you might have something that could help us find out what he was doing in Mont St. Michel, France, during the war." I also explained that Jack understood little or no German, and that I would translate everything she said for him.

Sister Beate sat there for a few minutes and said nothing. She closed her eyes and it seemed to me (though I had no real experience with the subject) that she was praying. Finally she opened her eyes and started telling her story.

Beate Schmiltz had grown up as the daughter of a privileged family. Before the war, life had been extremely good and her father's position in the army had guaranteed the family a comfortable life. She had been only nine when the war started, and that had changed everything. The privations of wartime, even for a privileged family, had been difficult, and had turned her to religion. After the German defeat in 1945, the revelations of what had taken place under the Nazi regime had horrified her and the thought that her father had been part of these horrors, even if "only" as an Army Officer, had changed her life forever. She entered a convent as soon as she could and had dedicated her life to relieving the sufferings of others. For many years she had worked as a nurse in various corners of the world, with famine sufferers and in Leper colonies, but about ten years ago she had been recalled to Germany to work in this hospice for terminal cancer patients.

"I have had very little contact with my family since I entered the convent in 1948. My brother Fritz seems to have died in France, just a few weeks after my father was killed on the Eastern Front, and my mother became unstable as a result. She was institutionalized for many years, and then mercifully died. I knew the Vollendorfs, of course – as a child, I saw them on family occasions, but I don't think I ever saw Max after the start of the war. My aunt Ingrid was an unpleasant person, but loved my father dearly, so we forgave her and helped her as much as we could during the war. She was killed in a bombing raid in 1944. As you know, the Vollendorfs had no children."

I nodded, quickly translated for Jack and said: "Thank you for this information Sister Beate. Do you know what happened to the Vollendorfs' possessions? I was hoping that some of his papers might have survived, which might help us solve the puzzle of what he was doing at Mont St. Michel."

Sister Beate thought for a moment and then said "When Tante Ingrid was killed, I remember that we went to her house – what was left of it – and collected bits and pieces of her belongings that had survived. Anything that was in one piece we took home with us, and put away in a little storage room in the attic. I assume that whatever there was would still be there, though I haven't been in that room for close to forty years."

"Do you still live in that house?" I asked.

"No, I live in a house in the town of Nikolausberg, just outside of the city, in a type of commune or dormitory with some of the other Sisters. It suits our very basic needs. The house I grew up in is rented out to some poor students at a very nominal sum. They occupy the first three floors of the house and the top floor is closed off. Whatever earthly possessions I had before entering the convent are still up there, along with my mother's and my brother's. There isn't much, and I have no use for any of them, but I have never bothered to dispose of them. I imagine that Tante Ingrid's things are there too, but as I said, I haven't been there in many, many years."

After bringing Jack up to speed again, he looked at me and cocked one eyebrow as if to say 'think we can go there?'

I had had the same thought, and asked Sister Beate: "Would you be willing to let us have a look at the room, and see if there is anything that might help us?"

"I don't see why not. I would like to help you find out what my uncle was doing, and perhaps pay some penance for his actions. I will go get you a key from my purse, it has always been on my key ring, and give you the address. When you are done – today, tomorrow or whenever – just please bring the key back, and you can leave it here at the desk with Inge", pointing to the receptionist.

"That is very kind of you Sister," I said. "I promise to return it as soon as we are done, and I will let you know if we find anything."

Jack nudged me and gave me the little book he had found in the rubble. "Oh" I added, "My cousin found this little book in the ruins of the tunnel in Mont St. Michel, and I haven't had a chance to look at it. It is in the old Gothic script, and I have a hard time reading that."

I handed it to her, and she began paging through it carefully. "This is a notebook of thoughts and ideas and is not very coherent. It's not a diary, it seems to be just random notes and bits of information. Would you like to leave it with me for a day or two, and when you bring the key back, I might be able to tell you more?"

I looked at Jack, who nodded very slightly, and said to Sister Beate: "Yes, Please. That would be very useful. I hope it is not too much trouble."

"No trouble at all, *junger Mann*." Here it was again, I was the eternal young man! "I have very little to do once I leave the hospice in the evenings, other than prayers and having meals, so this will be a change."

Sister Beate took a piece of paper from the reception desk, wrote the address of her family home on it and handed it to me. "The house was divided up many years ago into small one-room apartments, so you really shouldn't have any interaction with the residents. Just in case, I'll call one of the students right now, and let him know you are coming and that you will be going up to the third floor."

I thanked her again, and Jack made an effort to do the same in German, despite his total lack of knowledge of the language, and then we left. Jack's grandfather Nathan had gone to Canada from Germany in 1934, having seen the writing on the wall long before my grandfather. Unlike my Opa Ethan, he had abandoned his German heritage to the best of his abilities, and had married a Canadian-born Jewish girl from Montreal. Neither his son (Jack's father) nor his grandchildren (Jack and his brothers and sisters) could speak German, and they had little if any knowledge of German culture or history, other than the 1933-1945 aberration of Nazi Germany. Jack was 100% Canadian – Jewish, but first and foremost, Canadian.

# Chapter XV

The address on the piece of paper Sister Beate gave us was Herzberger Landsrasse 30, which we found to be about 2 kms away (I had picked up a city map at the train station while waiting for Jack this morning). We could easily have walked there in about 20 or 30 minutes, but I was anxious to get there, so we caught a passing taxi just outside the hospital.

A disheveled young man opened the door when we rang the bell (just out of courtesy, since we had a key) and welcomed us. "Sister Beate called and let me know you were coming. Please come in. My name is Thomas, and if you need anything, just let me know."

I thanked him, and then Jack and I started to climb the stairs. The house was old, the staircase steep and each floor was at least 20 or 21 stairs – far more than the modern norm of 16 or 17. By the time we got to the top of the house, we were both breathing heavily.

The last flight of stairs was dusty, and the carpet was worn thin. It was obvious that no one had been up these stairs for a long, long time. At the top was a door, with a heavy padlock that looked old and hand-made. I inserted the key that Sister Beate had given me and tried to turn it – with little success. The lock was old and rusted and obviously had not been used for many, many years.

I went back down the stairs (thinking about having to climb them again!), found Thomas and asked if he had any oil that might loosen the lock. He went into his room and came out again in a few seconds, holding a can of WD-40!

"Perfect" I said, "*Vielen Dank*", and went back up the stairs, huffing and puffing. By the time I reached the top, I was totally out of breath and could barely stand straight. I handed the can to Jack and croaked at him: "Try this".

He looked at me and said, "Sammy, you really should stop smoking!"

I threw him a look to kill and said "I never started – maybe I should now!"

Jack sprayed some of the solvent into the lock, waited 30 seconds and then reinserted the key and began to work it back and forth. Gradually it began to turn more and more, though with great reluctance and quite a bit of noise. Finally, it made a full turn to the right and the hasp of the lock opened.

Removing the lock, we pushed the door partially open, accompanied by some shrieking from the hinges. Forty or fifty years of disuse had done their job on the metal and it was protesting vigorously. I sprayed some more WD-40 on the hinges, and waited two minutes. Between the two of us, we then pushed the door open, and were greeted by a cloud of dust. The room had obviously been well sealed against the elements and opening the door had released the built up air.

The dust, and my huffing and puffing from climbing the stairs set me off in a paroxysm of coughing and Jack too joined in. It took us a few minutes to recover, by which time the dust had settled and we could see in. There was light coming from a skylight in the ceiling, which was lucky, as the light switch on the wall next to the door frame had no effect when turned. The room was packed with boxes and crates and some old furniture that looked like it had been dragged out of Ingrid Vollendorf's bombed-out house. It was obvious to me that searching the room would take quite some time, especially as we had no idea what we were looking for.

I sent Jack downstairs this time, to see if Thomas had a flash-light or lantern or something that would shed some light (literally) on the situation. "If he doesn't have anything, ask him where the nearest store is that might have one, and go buy something. Maybe a new light bulb will get the light to work."

"OK, Sammy, but don't blame me if the salesman doesn't understand me and I come back with a flame thrower instead of a flash-light!"

While Jack went in search of light, I sat down carefully on a dining-room chair that barely supported my weight, and took in my surroundings. I really didn't know what we were looking for, or where to start, but my instincts said it should be something military. I thought that Max von Vollendorf might have had a "foot locker" with his personal effects from his military service –

it would be logical that he did, and I only hoped that if he had had such a locker, it had been sent home to his widow after his death, and that it had survived the bombing of her house.

Jack returned after ten minutes, carrying a flash-light. "Thomas says we can use this, as long as the batteries last. He has no idea what shape they are in, it was left behind when a previous girlfriend moved out a few months back. He doesn't have a spare light bulb either."

With Jack holding the light, I began to explore the room. Every time I touched a box or a piece of furniture, a cloud of dust rose into the air, so I moved very slowly and carefully, touching as little as possible. "What we really need is an industrial vacuum cleaner" I said to Jack, "but I doubt that Thomas has one in his room. See if you can get that skylight open, and let in some real air."

Jack moved one of the old chairs under the skylight, stood on it and began playing with the skylight latch. Another quick spray of WD-40 and the latch released its hold on the frame, and he managed to push it open. The quality of air in the room improved immediately, as did the light level, since the skylight glass was grimy and less than transparent.

In order to make some sort of order in our search, we cleared a space by the one wall that was more-or-less accessible, and then began moving objects to this space that we didn't need to look through – like chairs and lamps. We then started on the various boxes – opening them to see what was in them. Boxes that contained dishes and other household items were stacked by the wall; those that held papers and personal items were put on a pile in the middle of the room. Once we had moved some of the furniture and household boxes to the wall, we had room to sit down and start going through the papers.

Jack went through the personal items mainly, as he couldn't read the German on the papers. I went through papers and discarded as many as I could without going through them too deeply – things like family letters, and old bills. My army experiences were nagging me, and I felt sure that Max must have had a box of personal items, and just hoped it had survived.

Finishing one box of Ingrid's school diplomas and prizes, I got up to get another cardboard box. When I picked it up, I saw behind it a wooden crate – or more exactly, a field-gray wooden box with rope handles at each end and two metal latches.

"Got it!" I cried. Jack came over and looked at what I had discovered.

"What's so special about a wooden box?" he asked.

"This is German Army field-gray, their standard color. It has to be somehow connected to Max."

"Couldn't it belong to the General – you know, what's-his-name, Ingrid's brother?"

I came back down to earth with a crash - "You're right, it might well be General Schmiltz's box, I totally forgot about him."

"Well, there's only one way to find out" Jack replied. He picked up the box, put it on a little table we had found, and pulled out the Swiss-Army knife that he always had in his pocket. The box had a small padlock on one of the latches, similar to the one that had been on the door. When he tried to open it by twisting one of the knife blades in the key-hole, the lock just crumbled into dust – it was rusted completely through.

Jack opened the box, accompanied by some minor resistance from the rusted hinges. It seemed to have been well sealed and protected against the elements, as there was very little dust inside and no smell of mold or rot. Inside, there were various items, which we laid out on the table as we took them out of the box. The contents were more or less what one would expect to find in a World War II German soldier's foot-locker: a shaving brush and straight razor, a stainless steel mirror, a dark green hand cranked dynamo flashlight (a Wehrmacht invention), some very yellow underwear, two pairs of woolen socks, a pair of steel-rimmed spectacles, a pair of leather gloves, and a very thick, black, leather-bound ring binder, with the word Tagebuch (diary) on the cover. The leather was dry, and crumbled when touched. After everything had been removed, we found pasted to the bottom of the box a piece of paper with an inscription, in hand-lettered Gothic print. It was a bit difficult to decipher, but I managed.

# Chapter XVI

**These are my personal possessions.**
**If anything should happen to me while serving**
**the Fatherland, I request that this box be sent**
**to my wife Ingrid von Vollendorf.**
**(signed) Capt. Max von Vollendorf**

There was a second field-gray box behind the first one, similar in style but almost a perfect cube in size and shape, but with no markings or identification on it. When we opened the box, we found a typewriter, with the Wehrmacht emblem on it. It had a label on the inside of the top, more or less identical to the one on the bottom of the first box.

I looked at Jack and said: "Naughty Max! Stealing a Wehrmacht typewriter!"

"I guess that all his possessions were shipped back to Ingrid when he was killed, and no one looked too closely at what they were."

When we opened the diary, we found this inscription, typewritten, on the front page:

```
The Diary of Max von Vollendorf, PhD
     Professor of Medieval History
   at the Georg-August-Universität
         Göttingen, Germany
```

After shouts of joy and great expectations, we turned the page and found that the diary was all typewritten on individual sheets of paper, presumably on the machine we had found.

I said to Jack: "Now you know how we are going to spend our evenings. This could give us answers to a lot of questions."

I closed the two crates, and put them to one side. Jack nodded, and we continued searching through the boxes in the attic room. Cartons of old clothing, incomplete sets of china and endless envelopes with letters were the final results after we finished going through the room – in addition to the furniture.

"I'll bet some stamp collector would love those envelopes" Jack said to me, "but it isn't worth while taking them with us now."

"No, and I'm not sure I want to read the contents" I replied.

"Me neither. I think we're done here, at least for today. Let's lock up and go see Sister Beate."

- - - - - - - - - - - - - - - - - - - -

We caught up with Sister Beate just as she was leaving the Hospice. When I showed her the diary, and explained how and where we had found it, she blanched a bit and said "Oh dear. I was afraid there would be something like this. Max was always writing in a notebook, and the one you gave me is very small and incoherent. I assume he transcribed his notes from little notebooks like the one you found in France, and typed them up for his diary. Are you finished going through the things already?"

"Yes, I think we are done. Do you have any objections to our reading the diary?" I asked, just as a formality. After all, it *was* her property.

She took another look at the diary, and said. "No objection at all. There is a lot here, and I don't really feel like reading it. To be perfectly honest, I really don't want to know what is in it – Max was an extremely strange man, and very unpleasant to be around. The last thing I want to read is his diary, and all his very private thoughts."

"I understand Sister. Would you have any objections if we took the entire foot-locker with us? I need to go back to Berlin tonight, and would like to go through everything carefully."

"By all means, take it all, and do what you want with it. I don't want it back. Oh, and I had a look at the notebook during my lunch break. It isn't very interesting, just notes on directions and quantities of earth. It sounds like he was leading an archeological expedition, but that can't be if this was written during the War."

I didn't comment on that, just nodded, and took the notebook from her outstretched hand. "If you are agreeable, we will take this notebook and the footlockers. If we find anything that concerns you or your family directly, I'll be sure to let you know."

"That's fine. Good luck to you both."

I suddenly remembered Sister Beate's brother – the one that was wanted for desertion. "Excuse me Sister Beate, but I have one more question. When we first met, you said that your brother Fritz seemed to have died in France. What exactly did you mean by that?"

Her eyes became very sad, and she said "Fritz had been a student of Romance Languages here at the university, and was 100% fluent in French. When he was called up for military service in 1941, they realized what an asset he was and he was sent to the occupied zone of France to work as a translator. In 1942 we received a telegram from the army saying that he was missing. We never heard anything more from them about Fritz, so we assumed that he was killed and maybe buried in France. In those chaotic days, it was not really possible to go chasing after army clerks to find out things like this. Fritz and I had been very close, despite the seven years difference in age, but I could not bring myself to find out any more details even after the end of the war."

I thanked her, and we left the Hospice. Out in the street, I turned to Jack and said: "I have an idea. We have nothing more to do here in Göttingen – why don't you come back with me tonight and spend some time in Berlin. I can read through the diary, you can take notes in English, and we can spend some time together, just 'hanging out'."

Jack jumped at the idea. "You're on. I have about ten days before my flight back to Canada, so why not spend it with you?"

"Just one more thing – we need to go back to the house, and take the foot-locker and the typewriter, but I really don't fancy traveling through Germany carrying a Wehrmacht foot-locker – it might give some people the wrong idea."

Jack nodded: "I noticed a store on the way here that looked like a small department store. We should be able to pick up some big duffel bags to put the boxes in – if your budget can handle that."

"Sure, that's no problem. And don't worry about my budget, it's all on the German Government's conscience."

We grabbed a cab on the corner and asked him to take us to the store, and wait for 10 minutes while we bought some bags. He had no objections, the meter would be running, and we quickly found the bags we wanted, and paid for them. He then took us back to the Schmiltz house, and we went back up the three flights of stairs. Jack held the duffel bags open, I put the foot-locker into the bigger bag, and the typewriter box into the smaller one. I had a last, quick look around, and saw a small pouch, like what we called a 'map case' that was also in field gray, and without even looking inside, put it into the bag with the typewriter box, and zipped it shut. I closed the door to the room behind me and locked the door.

We schlepped the two duffel bags back down the steps, knocked on Thomas's door to give him back the flashlight and the WD-40, and thanked him for his help, and then got back into the cab that took us back to the hostel. They had just opened the doors for the evening, and we quickly packed up our things and checked out. Jack paid the bill at the desk while I checked the train schedule. There were trains just about every half hour, and it would only take us about two and a half hours to get to Berlin.

The cab we had arrived in was still sitting outside the hostel, I guess business was slow that evening, so we climbed in and ten minutes later we were at the station. We had just missed the 18:03, so we grabbed a couple of sausages on the platform and caught the 18:43. It had been a pretty intense day, we were both tired, and within five minutes of leaving Göttingen we were sound asleep. We woke up as we pulled into the Hauptbahnhof in Berlin, grabbed a cab outside and 20 minutes later we were in my dorm room, where we put the two duffel bags into the wall closet. I had a spare bed, as during the academic year two students shared the room, so Jack just lay down on it, barely stopping to take off his shoes, and was asleep in seconds. It took me a few minutes longer, but I was soon asleep, dreaming of diaries and Max von Vollendorf.

# Chapter XVII
## *The Diary*

After we woke up the next morning and had breakfast, I took the foot-locker out of the duffel bag and had a look at the diary binder. All the pages were typewritten, but some were on different papers than others. The earliest entry was June 27$^{th}$, 1937, and the last one was for October 25$^{th}$, 1942. A quick look showed that there were not entries for every day, and sometime weeks, or even months, would pass between the entry dates.

Just reading through it would not be helpful, we needed to take notes and keep track of what was going on in Vollendorf's life. I decided on a course of action, and presented it to Jack.

"We need to have a better idea of what this guy was up to, and we need for you to be able to refer to it as well as me. So, I think we should proceed as follows: I'll read the diary entries one-by-one. Every time I come across an entry that appears to be of interest or value, I'll stop, go back to the beginning of that entry, and read it to you in a translated version. You can write up the translation on my laptop, as I read it to you, and you are welcome to make corrections to my English. How does that sound to you?"

"Sounds good to me," Jack replied. "I can't make heads or tails out of the German, even if it IS typewritten, so this works for me. I'll need the translations in any case, if any of it is relevant to my research. I'll include the date of the entry, so we will know where it comes from if need be."

"Great, so let's get to work." I opened the laptop, opened a new document and labeled it as "Max diary.doc" and saved it. My computer was set up to make automatic saves every five minutes while I worked on it, so I didn't need to worry about losing work.

We got to work immediately. I read the first entry, then read it to Jack in English, and he typed it into the laptop. The pages of the original were faint, and sometimes brittle from age, but in general I could read it all. Every so often there would be a word I didn't understand, and we would stop while I looked it up –

either on Google, or in a hard-copy German-English/English-German dictionary I had on my desk. In between the entries that I translated for Jack to type, I made some comments about the general tone of the diary and information that it contained, but that wasn't worth translating. There was a lot to be read between the lines – von Vollendorf had opinions on almost everything and everyone he came across. Progress was slow, and it certainly wasn't easy.

The first entry was short and to the point, and gave us a picture of what was to come:

*June 27ᵗʰ, 1937, Göttingen, Germany*

I am about to go to England to do research for my next book, and since I have never been there, I have decided to keep a diary, to record my impressions of that country.

The next few entries were similar, and seemed to set a pattern of what was to come.

*June 30ᵗʰ, 1937, Oxford, Great Britain*

I have just arrived in Oxford, having taken the ferry last night from Hoek van Holland, and then the train this morning from Harwich. The crossing was quite rough, and I was sick most of the way, and then all I could get to drink on the train was English Tea with milk! I was almost sick again. Such a strange habit.

The room I have booked is small, damp, and smells of cabbage, but I will manage, as I plan on spending most of my time at the university library.

Then he began his research. Britain didn't really suit von Vollendorf's character, and he vented a lot about England and English men and women:

*July 1st, 1937, Oxford, Great Britain*

This morning I went to the Bodleian Library in the center of Oxford, and I presented my credentials in order to begin my research. It was damp and cold outside, as one would expect in England, and the librarian was appropriately dressed in layers of stodgy woolen clothing.

I am to spend the summer here at Oxford University, researching old manuscripts at the Bodleian Library. The library's collection is unsurpassed in this field, and I hope to find answers to several questions that I posed in my last learned paper. These Englishmen have no idea what they have here and I will show them what true research is!

*July 5th, 1937, Oxford, Great Britain*

The woman who has rented the room to me is very unpleasant. I would like to find something better, but since I spend most of the day at the library, I don't know when I will find time to look for something else. I never have a penny for the gas meter and she refuses to help me with this. As a result the room is always cold and damp. Thank God the electricity doesn't work on these meters or I would be sitting in the dark whenever I was in my room.

Von Vollendorf seemed to have had a high opinion of himself, and a very low opinion of everyone else, and in general, everything that wasn't German.

*July 10ᵗʰ, 1937, Oxford, Great Britain*

While seated at a table on the second floor of the Bodleian this morning, I was reading a manuscript written in Medieval French - circa 1230. It is a beautifully illustrated document, complete with gold leaf and colored images, giving an account of the life of one Abbot Jordan of the Monastery of Mont St. Michel in Normandy.
My interest lies in the language of the document, and the illustrations it contains - not the contents. I hope to find materials here to prove my theory that German monks influenced the language of medieval French documents. Medieval French is a bastard language, and owes most of its limited beauty to Mittelhochdeutsch.

The little I knew about medieval languages came from an elective course I had taken during the third year of my BA program, and it seemed completely at odds with what von Vollendorf wrote. If anything, Mittelhochdeutsch was influenced by medieval French, and not the other way around. I certainly wasn't an expert on the subject, but I told Jack to type in a footnote at this point, to remind me to check this with one of my professors in Jerusalem, when I got back home. It didn't really seem important, but it just felt wrong and I wanted clarification.

*July 17th, 1937, Oxford, Great Britain*

I came upon another manuscript today, which has recently been added to the Bodleian collection. It comes from the monastery at St. Michael's Mount in Cornwall, in south-west England.

At this point, he wrote a whole page of background material on the history of St Michael's Mount and Mont-Saint-Michel. I didn't think it really important, so I skipped over it. His diary then continued:

The manuscript was a religious text, and as I leafed through it, a fragment of a page fell out. It was not part of the same manuscript - this was easy to tell as the writing was different in style and the color of the parchment was different too. The document contains bits and pieces of words in Medieval French, including the phrase *"... show the way from St. Michael to St. Michel"*.

The phrase caught my eye, and my interest. I know about both these monasteries: Mont St. Michel in Normandy, and St. Michael's Mount in Cornwall, from my studies and I have visited both of them in the past.

I know that there had been connections between these two monasteries, and exchanges of both letters and monks, but I know of no good reason for someone to use the phrase *"... show the way from St. Michael to St. Michel"* in a religious document.

It might have a maritime connection, but there is nothing else on the fragment to indicate that. The other words and fragments all have religious or monastic connotations, and there are no complete sentences, so the whole thing seems quite obscure.

As this is not connected to my immediate research, I have decided to leave it alone, and put it aside on the table.

The summer of 1937 passed without many more entries, and those that there were, were of little or no interest – mainly complaints about the British climate and character. At the end of September he returned to Germany. Then, on October 3rd, he wrote:

*October 3rd, 1937, Göttingen, Germany*

Upon my return to Germany last week, I went through all my notes and writing from the summer. Among the many papers and documents I gathered while working at the Bodleian, I discovered that I had inadvertently taken with me the fragment of the page with the references to St. Michael and St. Michel.

I thought perhaps to return it to the library in Oxford, but have decided against that. This is a piece of good fortune - no one will miss this fragment, as it was never properly cataloged in the first place. Perhaps I will be able to publish a paper on it. I shall call it 'the *St. Michel fragment*'.

Von Vollendorf's character starts to come out now – he isn't above stealing a document from the Bodleian Library, and justifying it to himself!

*Sunday, October 24ᵗʰ, 1937, Göttingen,*
*Germany*

I had some free time today, since my
students are all away on a Party-
sponsored weekend. After finishing my
preparations for next week's classes, I
decided to have a look at the '*St. Michel
fragment*'
The language is so vague, and the
document is in such poor condition, I
find it difficult to come to any
conclusions about it. I cannot decide
what it is talking about. Was this a
piece of correspondence between the two
monasteries? And if it was, what did it
mean?

It appears that von Vollendorf's academic principles and
credentials were not of the highest quality either. A picture was
becoming clear of a lone wolf academic, with delusions of
superiority and slightly neurotic. I began referring to him in
conversation as "Mad Max", and had to warn Jack not to use that
terminology in the translation.

*Sunday, November 21ˢᵗ,*

I have not shown the '*St. Michel
fragment*' to any of my colleagues in the
department. They are stupid and always
uncooperative - why should I share my
discovery with them? They will just steal
it and publish a paper before me. I spent
four hours last night in my office,
trying to read some more of the fragment.
I have even used a black-light on it, but
there is nothing else to be seen. How
utterly frustrating this is!

I went over to the French department last night. It was all dark and quite scary. No one was there, and those idiots never lock their doors. I spent some time in their library, but I could not find anything. At least I didn't have to be at home with that cow Ingrid. How could I have married her?

*Christmas Day, December 25th, 1937*

I could not wait for dinner to be over. Ingrid was stuffing herself with the goose and her horrible parents were there too. And her brother is now a colonel in the Army - it was all they could talk about - as if that were anything near as important as being a university professor!

*January 2nd, 1938*

I had a bit too much to drink last night, it was the only way I could get through the so-called festivities with the Schmiltz family. Such a bunch of country bumpkins. The only one that seems to have half a mind is Willi, and he looks down on me too. Not everyone can be two meters tall! But I had enough sense to leave the party while they were still drinking, and went to my study. I had not looked at the 'St. Michel fragment' for several months, and it seemed almost to be a new item - as if I had never seen it before! And then, suddenly, it came to me! Those monks knew of a secret way between Mont-Saint Michel, and St. Michael's Mount! That must be it!

There is a whole school of thought that says that we were visited by people from another world - how else could the pyramids in Egypt have been built? Perhaps they built a tunnel from one monastery to another? Could this be? Or did I have far too much to drink last night?

I stopped translating here and rolled my eyes at Jack. "Is this guy serious? Does he have any idea what he is talking about?"

"Sounds like a genuine nut-case to me" Jack replied. "Do you know how far it is from Mont-St.-Michel to Cornwall? About 300 kms, if not more! Even today no one has built a tunnel even half that length. As far as I know, the longest tunnel underwater that is big enough to be used for transportation is somewhere in Japan, and that is about 50kms long. This nut-bar had no idea what he was talking about."

I shook my head in wonder, and went back to the diary. This was getting weirder by the minute.

*March 5ᵗʰ, 1938*

I cannot rid my head of these thoughts about the monasteries. What a strange idea - that they could linked by a tunnel! If that existed, well, one could walk, or ride from France to England! Just think of it!

*April 10ᵗʰ, 1938*

I have just returned from a quick visit to Mont St. Michel, to see if I could find out anything about this tunnel. I found nothing to prove it or disprove it. The head of my department complained about my having missed a lecture I was supposed to give my class. Too bad, but my research is more important.

*June 23ʳᵈ, 1938*

This idea about the monasteries that I have could be vitally important to the Reich. All things point to the fact that one day soon we will be at war with those awful Englishmen, and this could help the war-effort. I must find a way of getting this information to the highest levels of the Party. Maybe Willi can help me with this - then marrying that woman will not have been a total waste. I must speak with him and see what he can do. He may be only an engineer, and a Lt. Colonel of *Pioniere*, but he does have connections in the party. How can I persuade him to help me - he looks at me like I am less than dirt. I need to catch him in a good mood.

Like all madmen that suffer from delusions, von Vollendorf had begun to hatch plots and plans. I think some professor of psychiatry would love to read this stuff!

*July 1ˢᵗ, 1938*

After dinner with Ingrid's foul family last night, I spoke to my brother-in-law. I said to him: "Willi, I have made an important discovery in my research, which could be useful, if not critical, to the future success of the Wehrmacht, and of the Third Reich."

He sneered and said: "*Ach so* - and what exactly is this discovery?"

I replied: "I can't tell you - it's so amazing and important that I can only tell it to someone of the highest rank. Someone that has the Führer's ear."

Schmiltz gave me a look that said 'you must be joking'.

"No, seriously!" I said, "I need to speak to someone from the inner-most circle, so that they can inform the Führer of this discovery."

Willi shook his head and tried to return to the dinner table, but I stopped him. "Willi, I'm not joking, and I'm not mad. I must speak to someone."

"Max - I do think you are mad, or even worse. I don't know why my sister married you, but even if you are now family of a sort, I'm not going to jeopardize my career for some insane notion you have."

"Please, Willi. I'm begging you. For the sake of the party, and the nation."

I was really desperate, and slightly drunk, otherwise I would not have had the courage to talk to him like this.

Finally, he said: "The only thing I'm prepared to do is to try and get you an invitation to a party next month, celebrating my commanding general's appointment to the General Staff. It's possible that Göring or Goebbels or Hess will be there, they've all been invited, and if you want to risk your career or your life, by trying to talk to one of them, well, on your head be it. But I can't promise that I'll manage, invitations for civilians are hard to get."

I said to him: "Thank you Willi. That will be very useful, and when the time comes, I'll put in a good word for you."

Willi shook his head, patted me on the
back like one would pat a loyal dog or a
precocious child, and returned to the
dinner table and his wife and mine. He
really is a horrible man, and that
uniform ill-becomes him. Maybe I won't
put in a good word when the time comes.
That will show him!

Jack looked up from his typing and said to me: "Do you sense a certain, shall we say ... flavor in his language?"

"I didn't want to say anything, but yes. He comes across as a real drama queen, doesn't he?"

"I think the word drama is superfluous – he's a flaming queen. I wonder how he survived in those days – the Nazis had a habit of killing off homosexuals, just like Jews."

"Yes," I replied, "but there was a really strange dichotomy in their attitude. On one hand, they imprisoned and killed homosexuals quite regularly, yet there are many reports and firsthand accounts of high-ranking Nazis that were closet homosexuals, and even some that were quite open about it."

"You've got to be kidding" Jack said, shaking his head.

"Yup – I mean, no, I'm not kidding, it's true. Maybe he got in with the right crowd, and that gave him protection from persecution."

"How do you know all this?" Jack asked.

"I have a good friend – he was actually the commander of my artillery piece in the army – who studied History with me at the Hebrew University, and he is gay. He was really shocked when this came up in some research he was doing – he said, it was enough to make him want to be straight!"

"Stranger and stranger," Jack said, and rolled his eyes.

I nodded and turned back to the diary to continue with the translation.

*August 7ᵗʰ, 1938.*

Willi Schmiltz has come through (only because Ingrid nagged him three times, after I nagged her - at least she is good for something), and an invitation has just arrived in our mailbox. It is addressed to Herr Professor Doktor Max von Vollendorf, and emblazoned with the Pionere Brigade's shoulder flash - quite beautiful actually and aesthetically pleasing. Much nicer than I would have expected from the Army. The invitation says: "Herr Professor Doktor Max von Vollendorf is invited to take part in the celebrations in honor of General Fritz von und zu Bergsdorf on the occasion of his appointment to the Wehrmacht General Staff."

I looked him up, and the General comes from a long line of barons and land owners in Pomerania, so he is real nobility and must have excellent connections. Perhaps I can talk with him about my project?

As this is a military occasion, the invitation is addressed only to me, as Herr Professor von Vollendorf, and Ingrid is not included. We had a nasty row over this, but there was nothing to be done about it - Thank God! Her behavior would be totally out of place and an embarrassment at such an occasion.

*August 28ᵗʰ, 1938*

I've packed my bags, including a dinner suit that had belonged to my father and fits me rather badly. Nothing to be done about that - there isn't time to order a new one, and it would be much too expensive. We never seem to have any money - that bitch Ingrid spends so much on clothes and restaurants. I leave in an hour for Berlin, the train is direct, and I should be there in plenty of time.

Willi Schmiltz made it clear that he wanted nothing to do with me, and has point-blank refused to even allow me to stay overnight in his house. What a horrible man he really is. I will have to make do with a somewhat seedy hotel near the train station (again, this lack of money is destroying me), and then take a taxi to the festivities.

*August 30th, 1938*

What a night that was! I have never felt so good in my entire life. The affair was in a mansion that belongs to General von und zu Bergsdorf. It has been his family's home for at least two hundred years, and looks like something out of a fairy tale. Towers poke up from every corner and there are between three and six stories, depending on which side of the house you are on. On the front were draped huge Army and National Flags, in Black, White and Red, stretching from the highest point down to street level. The party flag was strangely absent - the army still has not fully accepted the leading role of the Party in the life of the nation.

I saw Willi as I came in, but he ignored me completely and went off with some other officers. I wandered around, looking at the people who were there, and tried to find a personality that was high up in the party, that I could talk too.

After having a few glasses of Sekt, I walked into a side room and there was Rudolf Hess! He was sitting by the fire, with a champagne glass in his hand, and was reading a book.

I wasn't really sure how to behave with such a high-ranking official, and to tell the truth, my legs were shaking. But I knew that this was my one chance, so I just cleared my throat quite loudly and approached him. He looked up from his book and I said: "Forgive me Herr Deputy Führer, I hope I'm not disturbing you."

""Not at all," he said. "And you are..?"

"I am Professor Max von Vollendorf, of Göttingen University" I replied, and bowed deeply."

"Indeed. And did you come in to speak with me, or just to get away from the noise of this affair, like I did?"

"Actually, a little bit of both," I said. "I was looking for someone like yourself to speak with, and I really was not enjoying the party. It's not my style and not what I am used to."

"Ach so. It is not my favorite way of spending the evening either, but what can I do? It is part of my official responsibilities, so I show up, and then try to hide away. But you have found me, so what can I do for you, Herr Professor?"

I was still standing in front of him, between his chair and the fireplace, and getting very hot in the process, but he did not seem to notice, or care. "If I may explain ..."

"Go ahead" he said with a wave of his hand.

"I am a Professor of medieval languages. In the course of my research, I came upon an ancient manuscript, which seems to refer to a secret way between the monastery of Mont. St. Michel in Normandy, France, and the monastery of St. Michael's Mount, in England. I know this sounds outrageous and fanciful, but I believe it might well be true, and if it is true, then it could be of immense importance if the Reich were ever to be at war with England."

Hess looked at me quite seriously and asked: "How is this possible? It is a very great distance from Normandy to England?"

"I do not yet know how it is possible, but the document is quite specific, though it is not in good shape. I believe that beings from different worlds have visited this planet in the distant past, and this might be their work."

"I too believe we have been visited in the past. Please - sit down here and tell me more."

"Vielen Dank" I stammered and sat down on a stool near his armchair."

I gave him a short description of the document, and what I believed it meant. "If at some time in the future, the Reich will be at war with England, and we have the ability to reach Normandy with our troops, this would enable our forces to land in England without the British knowing about it in advance."

Hess sat still and listened to what I said. He refilled his glass with more of the Sekt and also a second glass, which he offered me.

"What do you know about this monastery in France? Is it likely that anyone there would know about this passageway?"

"Definitely not. I have been there not very long ago, the monks that run the monastery are a secluded group, they have very little contact with the outside world, and if such information were known, they would definitely have told someone about it. The last time I was there, after I returned from England, I wandered around the lower levels and could find no evidence of any passageway or tunnel. I was curious to see if there was any evidence for or against this document, but I could not find anything. There are, however, a number of stairwells that go down a few flights, but then come to a stop in front of a stone wall. I believe that behind one of these walls lie the answers to this question - it is just a question of finding the correct stairwell, and then to start digging."

"Tell me, Herr Professor, what would it require for you to find out more about this mysterious tunnel?"

I thought about this for a minute or two, and then replied very carefully: "In a theoretical situation, where the monastery would be under the control of the Reich, I could organize an expedition to uncover this tunnel. I would not need much in the way of funding or equipment, as the stairs and passageways are very narrow. If I were to have a dozen strong, able-bodied men, with pick-axes and shovels and wheelbarrows, we could quite quickly find out if there were any truth to this theory of mine. If the tunnel does exist, then it would probably be a major operation to clear it out. It would require reinforcements and pumps and things like that, having been abandoned for some 700 or 800 years!"

Hess shook his head. "If all this were to come about, that would mean that the Reich would be at war, and all our men would be needed in the Wehrmacht. We could not spare healthy men for such an expedition."

My heart fell. So near, and yet so far! And then I had a brainstorm. "We could use Jewish prisoners. There are bound to be some Jews with muscles, they can't all be bankers and rabbis. I'm sure they would much rather be digging a tunnel in France, than being in a concentration camp."

Hess smiled. "I like that idea! Let me make some inquiries and I will be in touch. It seems quite clear to me that we will be at war with England, and with France, within a year or two. When that happens, and this monastery is under German occupation, we can start working. I think that we should make this a Wehrmacht operation, so you will have to be inducted into the Pionere - the engineering battalions. I think you probably should be a Hauptman, so that there is no problem of authority when you are in charge of these prisoners."

I was totally in shock and could not believe what I heard. I had succeeded beyond my wildest dreams.

"How will we find these athletes?" I asked.

"Don't worry about it, I will get someone in the Pionere to do the work and find a dozen or so of these so-called athletes. We will arrange for them to be left alone, and not rounded up by the Gestapo. Once the monastery is in our hands, the Pionere will collect these men and send them to join you in Normandy. You will not need to do anything about the army, I will arrange everything. When the time comes, I will have a telegram sent to you with instructions."

"Thank you Herr Hess. Perhaps we have just made a huge contribution to the Reich's victory."

"Not so fast, Herr Professor, but I'm willing to try anything that will further our cause. Now, enough of business for tonight. Why don't we relax a bit? There are some interesting rooms upstairs, you might like them."

With that, he stood up, and guided me out of the room and up several flights of stairs. And I will not go into any details of what the rest of the evening had in store. That is a military secret!"

"Kinky," Jack said with a smirk. "But discrete. What a chance he took on talking with Hess – he must really have been obsessed with this crackpot scheme of his. He could just as easily have been arrested for "annoying the Deputy Führer" or something like that. Strange how there was no real security around Hess, they must have been so confident and felt so safe."

"Guess so. Look at the time – it's nearly four PM and we haven't had a bite to eat since breakfast. I need a break from all of this. Let's get a beer and anything that goes with a beer, and continue with this tomorrow."

"I'm with you. I'll just wash up and then we can go. By the way, didn't you meet anyone here at all that is your age and perhaps of the other sex?"

I smiled. "Believe me, if I had, I would have told you about it. Since I arrived from Jerusalem, I haven't had a single night out here in Berlin. The university is almost deserted due to the summer holidays and the places I've been visiting are like mausoleums – no one there except for skeleton staff. People just aren't interested in these things."

"Too bad, I could use some female company. All my volunteers at the Mont were either male, or married. And most of them were French! Never mind, I'll be with you in two minutes and then we can go out."

Half an hour later we were at a small bar just off the Kurfürstendamm, or "Ku'damm", as the city's main shopping street is colloquially known. "Tante Toni's" was a quiet little place, frequented mainly by students and known for its nice collection of beers. The place had an aroma that was part stale beer, part tobacco and part perfume, and the dozen or so little tables were full of young people – just what we needed.

As luck would have it, one of the tables had two empty seats next to two young students of the type Jack was looking for. After asking if they minded if we sat down (of course not) and if they spoke English (for Jack's sake – and they did), we placed our orders with a waitress that came running past – I had my regularly tipple, which was DAB, a great pilsner from Dortmund, and Jack had a Stella – the Belgian beer known world-wide.

I made the introductions and the girls were Ingrid (Germanistic studies) and Astrid (Art History). Of course they wanted to know what we were doing in Berlin, and I gave a much censored version of our adventures, leaving out the personal details and the nasty bits. They were both politely interested and I made sure I got both their emails and phone numbers before the night was over – not just out of personal interest (Jack pressured me hard to get them) but I thought we might need the services of one or both of them before our quest was over.

We made a 'date' of sorts to meet the girls the next night again, at the same *pinte* and left for the dorm by 10.

# Chapter XVIII

I dragged Jack out of bed at 8 the next morning, much against his will. I think the number of Stellas that he had the night before was more than what he was used to, as he groaned as he got up, held his head in both hands and stumbled into the bathroom. I had pity on him, and prepared a simple breakfast (orange juice, yoghurt and toast) in the room, rather than have my usual *Bauernfrühstuck* - a German farmer's breakfast, in the cafe around the corner – a large breakfast hash of potatoes and ham or bacon, with onions and peppers and some eggs mixed in. After his second cup of coffee (instant was all I had in the room), the color began to return to his cheeks and he managed to smile a bit.

"What did I drink last night?"

"Just a few beers, but I guess they were a few too many. Do you want some aspirin or Tylenol for your head?"

"No thanks. Another cup of coffee and I'll be OK."

I made it for him, and while he drank, got the diary out of my locked cupboard, turned on the laptop and was ready to go to work again.

*June 20th, 1940*

The French have surrendered! What wonderful news that is. Coming so soon after the Belgian capitulation, and the Dutch surrender on May 15th, this gives me hope that perhaps now my project will be able to start? I have not heard from Hess since our meeting almost two years ago, nor from anyone else in the army concerning the expedition - I hope he has not forgotten it. The road to Mont St. Michel is now open and I cannot wait to get there. I just hope that the Deputy Führer has not forgotten about my project.

Here came a number of pages that were dull and boring – just mundane notes about his life at the university and the occasional whine about how he had not heard from Hess. The university was running at half-speed or less, as more and more of the staff and students were called up into the army. From one or two of the entries it appeared that Max's colleagues were not overly complementary about his lack of military status. The entries were rare – usually no more than one or two a month, and I skipped over them, after asking Jack to make a notation about them in the translation. This period lasted from the end of June, 1940, till May 1941. Then came a bombshell.

*May 15th 1941*

I have just seen in the newspaper the shocking news about Hess's flight to Scotland. Can this be true? Is he really a madman or a traitor? This puts my Mont St. Michel project in danger. Will the Reich be able to win the war without it?

"Not over convinced of his own importance, is he?" Jack remarked. "He really was delusional."

"No question about it," I replied. "But see where it got him!"

*June 1st 1941*

This morning I received a letter in a large envelope from a Fraulein Freiberg. I have never heard of her, but when I opened it up, I discovered that she was Deputy Führer Hess's private secretary.

Her letter was short, and just told me that Hess had left instructions with her that in the case of something happening to him, she was to send me the packet of papers that were enclosed, together with the note from Hess.

The note was as follows - I have copied it word for word, the way Hess wrote it, and have burned the original!

To the honorable Prof. Dr. Max von Vollendorf:

If you have received this letter, it means that something has happened to me and that I will not be able to personally assist you in your extraordinary project. I have arranged for various papers and forms to be enclosed in this packet, none of which are dated. My trusted adjutant and close confidant, Oberstleutnant Dietrich von Fisher, knows all about the project and is a firm believer in its importance. Due to the difficulties of wartime, it is not possible to put the project into action at the time of this writing (April 1941), but as soon as it is possible, he will take all the necessary steps. You will know that it has been set in motion by receiving your induction notice into the Wehrmacht Pionere Corps. Everything else you will need is contained in the packet of papers.

Good luck, and I hope we meet again in Perfidious Albion, after the success of your project, and my mission.

Rudolph Hess, Deputy Führer of the German Reich

Jack and I looked at each other in disbelief. His reaction was: "No Shit!"

"More or less my feelings," I said. "This will make all sorts of historians go green – either from envy or from nausea. Too bad the nutcase burned the original; that would have been even better."

"You can't have everything. Amazing that not only Hess believed in this nonsense." With that, we went back to the diary. Another period of inaction and boredom came now, with only very occasional entries that were totally uninteresting. The letter from Hess's secretary and packet of papers had arrived in June of 1941, and von Vollendorf had had to wait impatiently for over a year, until the next act in this strange piece of Theater of the Absurd took place. June of 1942 brought with it big news.

*June 22nd, 1942*

Hurrah! This morning I received a telegram, ordering me to report for military service. I had given up hoping that this would happen. Ingrid is dumbfounded, she cannot believe that I will be in the army and has done nothing but say nasty things about me. An added bonus of being in the army is that I will not have to be around her any longer!

I packed a small case with underwear and my shaving kit, and a few other items, and said good-bye to Ingrid. She didn't even say good-bye back to me, and that, I hope, is the end of that.

*June 23rd, 1942*

When I presented myself at the Pionere base in Hanover this morning, I had no idea what to expect. A young, blond Leutnant received me and assisted me through the process of joining the Wehrmacht. I cannot imagine that all new soldiers are treated this way - it must be due to von Fisher's influence. I spent most of the day getting my uniforms, and then having them adjusted by the camp tailor to fit me perfectly.

*June 30th, 1942*

I have been so busy this week that I have not had time to write anything. Thank God today is Sunday and I have time to myself. Most of the week was spent learning about what it means to be a soldier, and what the Pionere are. I also spent half a day learning about rifles and pistols, and actually shooting them. They are very loud and I hope I never have to use one.

As a new soldier, I have only the rank of Gefreiter, but some of my instructors have let it be known that I will soon receive a different rank. This is very unusual, and must again be the work of von Fisher, carrying out Deputy Führer Hess's instructions. I would love to meet him sometime, and thank him for his help.

*July 15th, 1942*

I was called into the camp commandant's bureau this morning, and informed that from now on I will be a Sonderführer, and hold the rank of Hauptmann! I cannot believe it! Once again, I was sent to the camp tailor to get new uniforms. How splendid they are! This is like a dream come true!

Jack smirked. "All of a sudden army uniforms are OK with him! I thought he didn't like them."

I smiled back at him. "It all depends on your point of view I guess. Once he was in the army, it became, if you will excuse the expression, 'kosher'!

"Yech," was Jack's reply. "This guy has no ethics at all."

"I think we need a break – lunch sound good to you?"

Jack rolled his eyes, placed his hands in a position of prayer, and said meekly: "Yes, but no more beer – PLEASE!"

After a sandwich and a Fanta each, and buying a couple of chocolate bars for later, we returned to the dorm and got back to work.

*August 5ᵗʰ, 1942*

I am now home on leave for three days, before reporting for active duty. When I came into the house last night, and Ingrid saw me in my Hauptmann's uniform, she almost fainted! Her mouth dropped open so far you could have driven a car through it! She thought I had stolen the uniform, and when I finished telling her off, I showed her my *soldbuch* which lists my rank. The bitch was totally out of control, and shouted at me "Who did you have to sleep with to get that?" The nerve of the woman to doubt my honesty! I would have thrown her out of the house, but it is actually in her name, so I went up to my room and locked the door.

I think I will go back to the base tomorrow already, there is no point in staying here and being insulted by that woman.

*August 6ᵗʰ, 1942*

I returned this afternoon to the base. As I was walking to my room, the base commandant saw me and asked why I was back already. When I told him I preferred being on the base, he smiled, patted me on the back and said "That's a wonderful attitude for a soldier. Bravo."

*August 15ᵗʰ 1942*

The commandant called me into his office this morning and gave me my orders. I am to report to the Pionere base in Hamburg, where I will pick up my

group of laborers - he has no idea that
they are Jewish athletes who have been
rounded up from various locations and are
being held there.

*August 17ᵗʰ 1942*

On reporting to the Pionere base in
Hamburg-Altona, I found a sealed envelope
waiting for me in the adjutant's office.
In it was a short letter from
Oberstleutnant Dietrich von Fisher, in
which he informed me that there were 12
Jewish athletes in the base lock-up, who
were at my disposal. They are mine to
deal with as I saw fit, for any project
that would benefit the Reich. I was not
to worry about anything happening to
them, as they no longer officially
existed. All their papers had been
destroyed, and there was no record of
them having been arrested or transported
or anything like that. There were also
some other forms and papers.

I was to take the men, plus a *Feldwebel*
(Sergeant) from the Home Guard who was
already waiting for me at the base, and
proceed directly to Mont St. Michel. I
was to send a report to von Fisher at the
Reich Chancellery in Berlin if and when I
had anything important to report. I was
allowed to requisition light equipment
such as shovels and wheelbarrows from the
Pionere Base, but nothing more than that.
A two-tonne truck was at my disposal, to
get the prisoners and the equipment to
Mont St. Michel, as was a Kübelwagen for
myself and the Feldwebel.

I presented myself and the letter to the base adjutant. He scowled at me, but when he saw who the letter was from his attitude changed, clicked his heels and said "Jawohl, Herr Hauptmann." He gave orders to his clerk to find the Feldwebel, to get the vehicles ready and load the equipment. Then he asked me to follow him and we walked across the parade ground to a bleak, concrete block building.

Here I had my first meeting with my prisoners. They all looked athletic but undernourished. On the other hand, so were many citizens of the Reich - food was starting to become scarce. They were shackled hand to hand and foot to foot.

They said nothing to me, and looked a bit dazed and afraid, and that was fine with me. I didn't want any trouble with them, all I wanted was for them to dig where I told them to. I asked the adjutant to unshackle their feet, and get them on the truck with whatever possessions they had, as I was anxious to get going. The camp supplied me with a driver, since the truck was only for getting to the site. After delivering the prisoners to the site, the truck would return to the base, as it was needed for the war effort. The Feldwebel showed up with the Kübelwagen, and I was a bit taken aback, as he appeared to be at least 50 years old, if not more, and quite overweight. I just hoped he would never have to run after any of the prisoners, or fight with them hand-to-hand. He saluted properly though, his uniform was perfect, and he held the door of the vehicle open for me to get in. Once I was seated in the back, he picked up my bags, put them into the second front seat and started the car. We pulled out of the base, with the truck behind us, and headed west out of the city.

During the first stage of the trip, I made sure he knew where we were going, and that he had the proper maps. All was in order, and it appeared that Oberstleutnant von Fisher had made all the necessary preparations. I was amazed that he had bothered with all these details by himself - I'm sure he had more important things to do than arrange for my little expedition, but it showed me that he believed in it, and that he was aware of its potential importance. Now that Hess was out of the picture, it was important that someone else believed in the project and was around to deal with the details.

Among the papers I had received together with the letter from Deputy Führer Hess was a program for the trip we were taking. It listed the various bases where we were supposed to overnight along the way, and included vouchers for the rooms and meals for myself and the Feldwebel. The prisoners would sleep in the truck, and eat field rations, like the soldiers at the front. They would probably be happy to have them, food at the Pionere base lock-up in Hamburg would not have been anything special, I'm sure, and I didn't know how long they had already been there.

*August 18ᵗʰ 1942*

Last night we slept at a Luftwaffe base
in Osnabruck. I made sure that the
Feldwebel was up by 06:00 and we were out
of there by 07:00. Our reception there
was less than warm, and I wanted to get
away as quickly as possible. Before we
left, I took the Feldwebel aside and told
him that I needed a typewriter for
writing my reports. I didn't have a
requisition voucher for one, so I told
him to try and obtain one by any means
possible. Hess or von Fisher really
should have thought about this, but they
hadn't. He looked at me as if I had asked
him to rob the Reichsbank, but didn't say
anything.

"Why am I not surprised?" I said to Jack. "He must have felt
like a Hassid at a Catholic wedding."

"Nice comparison, Sammy. Those Luftwaffe types probably
had fun with him and his side-kick the sergeant"

*August 19ᵗʰ 1942*

We slept last night at an Artillery
base outside of Dusseldorf. I don't know
if this is on purpose, and if so why, but
we are not spending two consecutive
nights in bases belonging to the same
branch of the armed forces.
In the morning, as I was getting into
the Kübelwagen, the Feldwebel showed up
with a square wooden crate, painted
field-gray. He handed it to me once I was
seated, saying "Zu befehl", and then got
behind the wheel. Once we were under way,
I opened the crate and in it was a
Wehrmacht typewriter! "Well done" I said

to him, and he saluted, even though he was looking forward and not at me.

"I guess that not even Hess or von Fisher felt completely at ease with this project and wanted to keep it as quiet as possible. Not letting this motley crew spend two nights in the same place was probably just a cautionary tactic."

The next few pages just talked about where they slept each night, so I told Jack to make a list of the locations and I skipped to the next interesting pages.

• *August 20ᵗʰ 1942.* Last night we spent at former Belgian Army base near Charleroi (Belgium)

• *August 21ˢᵗ 1942.* An ex-French infantry base, now occupied by the German military government for the area, just outside of Amien (France)

• *August 22st 1942.* A Wehrmacht forward base in Rouen.

*August 23ʳᵈ 1942*

Mont St. Michel at last. The tide was up when we arrived this morning, but we still managed to get across the causeway. In the village we found a house that looked like it was abandoned, and unpacked our things there. It wasn't very big, but I wasn't concerned about the comfort of the prisoners - they weren't there for a holiday. I had the Feldwebel gather them in the main room of the house, and explained the situation to them. We were going to undertake an archeological exploration underneath the monastery which was part of the war effort. As long as they behaved themselves, and did what they were told to do, they would be safe and protected. They could not work if they were chained to each other or in handcuffs, so they would be on the 'honor system'. Anyone attempting to escape would be shot on the spot, and I assured them that the Feldwebel, despite his age, was an expert shot. The Feldwebel looked at me and nodded in agreement. If they behaved and worked hard, their life with me would be decent and agreeable. If not … I left the sentence hanging, and I am sure that they understood my meaning.

I left them to get their room at the top of the house organized and sent the Feldwebel out to gather some more furniture and see about provisions. I had some blank requisition orders from the packet from Herr Hess, and I told him to use them sparingly, since once they were used up, we would have to acquire things by force, and I wanted to avoid that as much as possible.

He came back after an hour, accompanied by a woman. He told me he had arranged for her to cook for us and the prisoners, and in return we would make sure her husband's bakery was protected. I wasn't sure what I could do about the bakery, but it sounded like a good arrangement. He went out again with four of the prisoners to bring back some furniture on the Kübelwagen They walked while he drove, but there wasn't much difference in their speeds, considering the narrow lanes of the village.

We spent the rest of the day getting the house arranged, and I walked up to the Monastery, to get reacquainted with it. It was the same as I remembered it, the only difference being that there were no real tourists walking about. The only ones there were some Wehrmacht soldiers, and when I asked them, they told me they were from the garrison at Avranches, just up the coast.

I took that opportunity to take a letter from von Fisher I had in my map-case, and told their Leutnant to give it to the garrison commandant in Avranches, so that he would a) know that we were here, and b) that what we were doing was official Reich business.

In the evening, I took out the typewriter for the first time, and started to type up this diary, starting at the very beginning when I sailed to England. I hope to type up all the back pages in the evenings, after dinner, when we are done with our day's work.

*August 24ᵗʰ 1942*

This morning I took my troop of prisoners together with the Feldwebel, and we went up to the Monastery. I stopped the first monk I found there and asked to be taken to the Abbot. When we got there, I presented him with another letter from von Fisher, which told him in French that we were there on official business, that we would be conducting an archeological dig in the abbey and that they were under no circumstances to hinder our work, if they wished to be otherwise left alone. He was very upset, but realized that there was no point in arguing, and left the room while muttering under his breath.

I could now start work. I told the Feldwebel to get the equipment and bring in into the Abbey. I took one of the prisoners with me, and started to explore the stairwells, trying to find one with the best chances of being the mystery tunnel. I had a soldier's compass and used it to get a bearing on what I took to be the general direction of England. We went down the stairwell that was closest to the northern corner of the abbey, and started to look. I explained to the prisoner that we were looking for a tunnel that went down from the end of one of the stairwells and that he should help me with this.

*August 27ᵗʰ 1942*

I have decided that stairwell no. 3, in the most north-eastern corner of the abbey, is the most likely to be the one we are looking for. The first five flights of steps are in good order and seem to have been used often. There are some rooms and passageways leading off of some of them. The next nine flights of steps are in worse condition and don't seem to have been used much. From the bottom of the last flight, there is a tunnel that slopes down, and then after four or five meters it comes to an end. This seems to be the best spot to start digging.

"Hey," I said to Jack. "This sound just like your description of when you started digging."

"It sure does. Guess it's the same stairwell we worked on. Looks like everything is beginning to fall into place."

*August 28ᵗʰ 1942*

We have brought all the equipment down the stairs, to the point where the passageway is walled up. The prisoners have been organized into 'diggers' and 'haulers'. The two strongest ones are to work at the face of the tunnel, digging away at the rubble that fills up the tunnel, and the rest will haul away what they loosen. We will have to figure out a way of getting the rubble up out of the stairwell, otherwise there will be no room to move in a very short while.

*September 5ᵗʰ, 1942*

I have decided that we will use a passageway on the 8ᵗʰ level of steps to store the rubble the prisoners are removing. I estimate that there is enough room there for about 10 to 15 meters of tunnel excavations. By the time we finish that much, we should have a better idea of what awaits us.

*September 13ᵗʰ 1942*

The prisoners are very grumpy, and are not in the best of shape. In order to keep them happy, I have allowed them to go running on the mainland - one by one. I have told them that the condition of this parole is that if one of them runs

112

away and doesn't come back, all the rest will be shot immediately. I don't care how they arrange this, but I have made it clear to them that this is not something that is negotiable. I realised they need the release, in order to work better, but I am not going to endanger the entire project.

Since today is Sunday, I have told them that they have half a day off and that one of them may go for a run. I warned them again not to even think about escaping. The rest are to remain in the main room on the ground floor. The Feldwebel is stationed there with his very obviously loaded Schmeisser MP38. The men drew straws and one of them immediately stripped down and ran out the door and down to the causeway.

*September 20th 1942*

We have settled into a kind of routine. During the day the prisoners dig and remove rubble, and I supervise them. The feldwebel is in charge of seeing to it that we have supplies and meals. On occasion he comes to the dig site so that I can have a break, but climbing up and down the stairs seems to be very difficult for him and so I try to keep this to a minimum. I don't understand how someone in his physical condition could have been drafted into the army.

In the evenings, I sit in the room and type up this diary. I make sure that every hand-written page that I type up is then burned, so that there is no chance of this information being stolen. The typewritten version I keep in my foot-locker, under lock and key.

*September 27ᵗʰ 1942*

I have not written anything new in this diary for two weeks, as there has been nothing to report. The work in the tunnel is going very slowly, for several reasons. The rubble is very tightly packed and is hard to remove. There is so little room there that it is hard for the prisoners to get in to remove it, and then carry it up the stairs. And the prisoners are getting weaker by the day, due to the hard work and lack of sufficient food. I almost feel sorry for them, but then I remember who (or what) they are, and that this is all for the greater good of the Third Reich. I've told the Feldwebel to take the Kübelwagen tomorrow and go for a drive on the mainland, to see if he can't find some better food supplies to requisition.

*October 11ᵗʰ 1942*

We are all getting weak from the efforts involved in the project. I of course am not doing any of the physical labor, but all the walking and climbing and up and down on the stairs is taking its toll on me. I have never been an athletic type, and this project is very hard for me.

The prisoners are becoming unruly, too, which is problematic. One of them had the nerve to stop work in the middle of his digging shift and demand to know what we were doing. I put a swift end to that, slapped him hard with my leather glove and pushed him back to the tunnel. In normal times he probably could have broken me in two with his bare hands, but he like all the others is very weak now. I screamed at him to get back to work, and warned them all of the dire consequences of not working as they should. I told the Feldwebel to fire a few rounds from his machine pistol, as a warning, but they had a terrible effect. The noise in the tunnel was fierce, and the bullets bounced off the rock walls again and again. One of the prisoners was hit by one of the bullets, and had to be taken back to the house for treatment.

I fear that the prisoners' usefulness is coming to an end, and I don't know what to do about it. I have written a letter to von Fisher, telling him that I need more men and that I will soon need to get rid of the current group in one way or another. The Feldwebel took the letter to the Avranche garrison for mailing to Berlin, but I honestly don't expect a reply. The war is not going as well as the Fuerher expected and finding men to work on my project is going to be difficult.

*October 28ᵗʰ 1942*

We are all hungry all the time now, and I don't know what to do about it. The men are very weak and as a result the digging is going very slowly. I can't really blame them for not working as fast as I would like, but we need to progress somehow. Finding the tunnel could change the whole course of the war, but no one seems to care.

*November 26ᵗʰ 1942*

After dinner this evening, I told the Feldwebel that he must go tomorrow to the garrison in Avranches, and see if he cannot get some field rations or other food supplies. What we have is not enough to keep the prisoners digging, and both of us have lost a lot of weight. I'm sure the soldiers on the front have no more to eat than we do, but our project is so critical to the success of the war-effort, that they really need to get us supplies. I don't have much hope for my 'mission' any more, but I must try.

I gave him my pistol, and have taken the Schmeisser from him, so that I will have something to control the prisoners if they become unruly again. I hope he finds some supplies in Avranches, so that when we are done for the day, we will have something substantial to eat.

That was the last entry in the diary. After reading Mad Max's diary (that's how I had begun thinking of this obviously insane German), I had a new perspective on the findings in Jack's tunnel. I discussed it with Jack, over a few beers in a local *pinte* in Berlin.

"I guess that he must have been killed some time soon after this last entry, since he was pretty steady in his writings, and seems to have finished transcribing all of his hand-written diary pages. We now have a reasonable idea of what von Vollendorf was doing in Mont St. Michel. He obviously thought that he was going to win the war, single-handedly, by finding a way to get German troops into England, without anyone being the wiser."

Jack nodded. "What a nutter! He had no concept of geography, or basic engineering, or just plain common sense. He was truly delusional."

"Agreed," I said. "I think we need to go back to the Mount. I still have many questions about this whole affair, and the answers, if they exist, must be there. Remember the spooky waiter? He said we should try some cafe in St. Malo."

"I think you're right, Sammy. And I'm thrilled that you've jumped in on this. Without your historian's knowledge and perspective, and your research in Germany, I'd still be where I was when you first showed up. When we finally get to the bottom of the whole story, we'll write a paper together. I still have a week to go before I should be back at university, and even if I'm late, nothing will happen. I'm not teaching this semester, so there is no problem."

"Done!" I said, and we raised a glass of beer in a toast. "So back we go to Normandy. I'll check the schedule to St. Malo when we get back to the dorm, and we can catch a train in the morning. Nothing more to keep us in Berlin for now."

"Right. And see if you can find a hotel of some sort there, I'm getting to old for youth hostels."

"Wimp! You should have seen some of the places I slept in during my military service."

"Thanks – but no thanks. Jack is a pampered Canadian, who likes his creature comforts."

# Chapter XIX
## M. Daniel's Story

It was a sunny Sunday afternoon when we arrived in St. Malo and checked into the hotel I had booked online. In the old town, near the water's edge, across the street from the sea-wall, we found our goal. At the Café de la Liberation, the average age of the clientele was over 70 – well over, in fact. Some of the men looked as if they had been sitting in the same spot since the liberation of St. Malo in 1944 – dark blue berets on their heads, Gauloises cigarettes hanging from their bottom lips as if glued there, and a glass of *marc* on a 2-franc saucer (though the price today would have been probably closer to 20 francs – if francs were still the currency of France, and not Euros) and the saucers looked like they hadn't been washed since the fall of France in 1940!)

Some of the patrons looked up as we entered, but most of them couldn't be bothered. Jack motioned me to follow him, and we walked up to the brass bar. He ordered two *blondes* (lager beers), and when they arrived, tipped the barman generously and started talking with him, explaining who he was and that he was in charge of the "dig" at Mont St. Michel. I was worried that my high-school French wouldn't allow me to keep up, but I surprised myself by understanding most of what I heard. Before we had walked in, I had asked Jack to keep the conversation at a level I might be able to follow, and he was doing his best.

Jack asked the barman. "Is there anyone around – perhaps one of your customers – who was here during the occupation? I'm trying to find out something about that time."

The barman swept his hand around the room and said, "Take your pick. 90% of my clientele were in the *résistance*. What do you want to know?"

"I want to talk with someone who was in or around Mont St. Michel during the war. Were any of them there?"

He thought for a moment, then pointed to a table in a back corner of the room. "Try M. Daniel, at the last table – and take him a glass of red wine if you want him to like you."

Jack thought a minute and then asked for a bottle of good red wine – "not *vin ordinaire!*" Having paid for it (again with a generous *pourboire*), we took three glasses and ambled over to the back table. The man sitting there was dressed like all the others, except that his right sleeve was empty and folded up to near his shoulder.

"M. Daniel?" Jack asked the old man. He nodded, but said nothing. Jack tried again. "Can we sit down? We'd like to talk with you." "The old man nodded again. Jack placed the bottle of wine (a Cote du Rhone 2003) on the table and I added the glasses. M. Daniel's eye sparkled ever so slightly when he saw the label. I guessed it was not his regular drink, and poured him a glass. While Jack and I were getting seated, the old man lifted the glass, held it up to the light, smiled with genuine delight, and then to my complete and utter amazement, opened his mouth and pronounced quietly: *"Baruch Ata Adonai, Elohenu Melech HaOlam, Borei Pri HaGafen."*

The last thing I would have expected to hear in a St. Malo café was the traditional Jewish blessing over wine. Jack and I exchanged looks of total surprise, and then both of us started talking at once, me throwing questions at Jack, and Jack at the old man.

Over most of the bottle of wine, it came out that M. Daniel (full name Daniel Haas) was the product of a Jewish father and a Catholic mother. In the thirties in France, being Jewish was not much better than in Germany, and he was brought up nominally Catholic, with the rudiments of a basic Jewish education from his father. He managed to hide his origins during the German occupation, and early on joined the Resistance. He finished his third glass and asked us what we wanted of him.

After introducing ourselves and explaining our origins, we came to the question of the Monastery and the helmet. A strange, far-away look came over him, and he became quiet and reflective. Jack went back to the bar and returned with another bottle of Cote-du-Rhone. M. Daniel poured himself a glass, but this time started to recite the *mourner's Kaddish* – the Jewish prayer for the dead. My capacity for astonishment had now overloaded and I didn't know what to say. Jack looked at M.

Daniel as if he had lost his mind, but managed to keep his opinion to himself.

When the prayer was over, the old man looked at us and said "I've kept this story to myself for 50 years, and I suppose it's time it came out."

At our look of perplexity, he began his tale. He was born in St. Malo, but at the time of the occupation he was working in a bakery in the village below the monastery. One day in 1942, a truck and a staff car arrived at the monastery. The German garrison was installed in Avranches, but these vehicles came from somewhere else. The staff car contained an elderly sergeant-driver and a diminutive, bespectacled Captain, and the truck disgorged a motley crew of civilians – all large, and athletic looking, though underfed and bewildered. The Captain took over an abandoned house, and the men were billeted in the attic. One of the Captain's first acts after arriving was to arrange for the local bakery to supply large quantities of bread to the men. He also requisitioned supplies of sugar and meat – whatever could be found. At the beginning there were still reasonable supplies available and though there were many complaints from the locals, he managed to obtain most of what he demanded.

Every morning the sergeant would collect the men from their house and march them up to the monastery. They would enter through a side door, and reappear in the evening, going back to their house. A local woman was hired to cook for them, and was told never, ever to ask any questions, or even speak to the men, under pain of arrest and imprisonment. M. Daniel would deliver bread from the bakery to their house every morning before they left for the monastery. The men were obviously prisoners of some sort, but their conditions were lax, to say the least, and the relations between the old sergeant and these men were correct, if not pleasant. Certainly not the normal jailer/prisoner arrangement. M. Daniel would see them only in the mornings, as bakers work from 4am to 12 noon, and then go home to sleep.

One late Sunday afternoon he was walking past the men's house and one of the prisoners came out – alone. To M. Daniel's surprise, the man was wearing shorts and a singlet. The man did some quick stretching exercises and then set off at a loping pace, down the winding streets of the village and out onto the causeway connecting the monastery with the mainland. He (M. Daniel) was convinced that the prisoner was escaping, and quickly went looking for the local resistance leader, to try and assist the man. However, an hour later he was astounded to see the man return up the street, still running and dripping with sweat, and enter the house.

On orders from the resistance, M. Daniel began surveillance of the house, and soon learned that this was a common event. Different men would come out in the late afternoons or evenings, run down the street and over the causeway, returning at least one hour later. The timing of their runs depended on the tides, as the causeway was often flooded at high-tide and dangerous to cross. The resistance members were puzzled, to say the least, by this behavior. To their way of thinking, any prisoner of the Germans that had such an opportunity would and should naturally take it to flee, and not return. After consultation among the local members, it was decided that M. Daniel would try to find out what the story here was – by joining one of the men on their run. M. Daniel was chosen because a) he had first discovered the phenomena, and b) he was best suited to the task, having been a local athlete before the war.

On a gloomy afternoon, M. Daniel waited at the bottom of the street for one of the men to appear. The prisoner ran down the street and onto the causeway and M. Daniel started after him, keeping a distance between them until they were on the mainland and out of sight of the monastery. On a country lane, far from any habitation, M. Daniel caught up with the runner and forced him off the road. When the man started to shout and berate him for causing an 'accident', M. Daniel clamped a hand over his mouth, pulled a pistol from his pocket and pointed it at the man. "I want to know exactly what you are doing, and what is going on in the Monastery, and you are going to tell me. Otherwise, I will use this gun and you will do your next run between St. Peter and the pearly gates!"

The pistol was enough persuasion and the runner told all. The men were all Jewish and all former athletes. They had been identified by the army long before the invasion of France, picked up, warned to keep their mouths shut and to stay fit – if they wanted to survive. All they had been told was that they "had been chosen to perform an important service for the Third Reich". If they cooperated, they would be protected persons, that the Gestapo would not come for them and that they would be given odd jobs to keep alive. All that they were required to do was keep in good physical shape and when the time came, they would be asked to assist the Reich in an important project.

When I heard this I gave a shout, and everyone in the café looked at me as if I were mad. This was the same story that Herr von Marburg back in Berlin had told me about my uncle Samuel.

I apologized for the intrusion, and motioned to M. Daniel to continue. He took another sip of his wine, thought for a minute and continued. The athlete explained that the men took turns running at odd times, in order to keep in shape. When asked why they didn't escape, he explained about the 'arrangement' – that the escape of any one of the athletes would bring about the immediate execution of the rest. During the day, they were working in the lower levels of the monastery, digging out a tunnel. They were not told what they were doing, or why, just given orders where to dig.

M. Daniel let the man get up, with a stern warning not to mention their meeting to anyone. The prisoner ran off and M. Daniel returned to his lodgings. Later in the evening he met with his resistance comrades and told them what he had learned. The story was debated hotly, as it did not ring 100% true, but in the end they agreed to leave things as they were – for the time being.

"And?" I asked. "What happened after that?"

"We continued to monitor the prisoners, but there was little or no change in their routine. This went on through October and into November. On occasion, I would track the same prisoner as I had stopped the first time, run out with him onto the mainland and stop him someplace secluded. I always made sure to have a piece of bread or something to give him, and we would talk for a few minutes. He reported that they were still digging, it was a long, long tunnel going down beneath the Abbey and that they still had no idea what they were doing, or why. The little Captain that was in charge refused to tell them anything, and would become hysterical if they questioned him. The men were getting weaker, despite their athletic efforts, since the food they received became less and less."

"Late in 1942 – I think it was November" continued M. Daniel, "an allied bomber flew over the bay, presumably on its way back from a raid in Central France. It must have been damaged on the way, because it was flying low and trailing smoke. As it passed over the area, it dropped a bomb, probably in an attempt to lose weight and gain altitude. The bomb fell in the sea immediately adjoining the Mount, and landed at the juncture of the monastery wall near the tunnel. The monks were afraid that the foundations had been damaged, and went down the stairs to check. When they got to the bottom, they found that the bomb had caused the tunnel to collapse onto the men working there."

"In the village we had heard the bomb go off, but didn't know what damage it had caused, until one of the monks from the monastery came to get me. He knew I was connected to the resistance, so he contacted me for help. He didn't know what to do with the body of the Captain and thought I might have some ideas."

"I took part in the rescue efforts, which were in fact only recovery operations. Everyone that had been in the tunnel at the time of the bombing was killed. We found two bodies in the stairwell leading to the tunnel – one was the German Captain, and the other, one of the athletes. It appeared that after the bombing, the Captain must have gone mad, and collapsed the last wall on purpose, in an attempt to hide the project and leaving all evidence of the digging inside the tunnel. If any of the prisoners managed to survive the bombing, this would have killed them. One of the athletes had managed to get through, and had attacked the Captain for what he had done, killing him but dying in the process. There was a Schmeisser machine pistol lying by their bodies, and both bodies had been shot many times. There was an old model Schmeisser that would go off suddenly if dropped, and it looked like this was what happened."

The old man's eyes teared slightly, even after all these years. "When I turned the body over, I saw it was the prisoner I had followed – the one that originally told me what was going on. We dug through the rubble and reached the bodies of the other prisoners, and then buried them in the local graveyard at the foot of the Mount. I arranged for the Captain's body to be sent to the local German garrison, accompanied by the old sergeant who had been in charge of guarding them. When the bomb exploded, he had been away and not in the tunnel – I don't know why, and I didn't ask. He was warned by us that if he were to give any information about the resistance to the garrison, we would know where to find him, but if truth be told, he seemed to be totally at ease with the events and not at all interested in the resistance. I think he just wanted to go home, he was obviously much too old to be involved with actual fighting. He took down in a notebook a description of what had happened, dictated by the resistance. Strangely enough, there was never any reaction from the garrison, no reprisals, no investigation, *rien du tout*."

My mind was working in overdrive after hearing his story and I could barely contain myself, Questions kept popping up in my head and I wanted to get them out before anything happened or I forgot them!

"M. Daniel", I said, "Did you ever learn any of the men's names? Are they buried in individual graves or all together? Did anyone check their rooms to see what they left behind?"

"*Lentement*, mon ami!" he replied. "Slowly, one question at a time. I'm an old man and I cannot keep up with you."

"*Pardon*, M. Daniel," I replied, "Please forgive my enthusiasm and bad manners."

Jack, who had been sitting by the side, drinking in the whole amazing story, said "Perhaps you would like to take a break and have some lunch, M. Daniel?"

"*Merci*," he replied, "That is very kind of you."

I got up and went over to the metal bar counter and asked the barman what there was to eat. The choice was limited, the typical basic French café menu of baguettes with Camembert cheese or *Jambon* – French ham. I instinctively chose the cheese over the ham, even though I have no religious or cultural issues with eating pork. Perhaps M. Daniel didn't care either, but cheese was safer. I asked the barman for six of the sandwiches (they weren't huge, and I was really hungry by then), and when they were ready, I brought them over.

Back at the table Jack and M. Daniel had finished the second bottle of wine. This was not my normal lunch drink – orange juice or water were more the Israeli style, but this was the local custom and I did my best to keep up. M. Daniel looked at the sandwiches, smiled, and dug in with a gusto that belied his years.

Jack and I finished our two sandwiches each while M. Daniel worked on his. After one and a half he gave up and pushed his plate away. "I'm not the man I used to be" he said with a grin.

"Now, to your questions. After we buried the men, I went with some of the other members of the resistance to the house where the men had been quartered. The first thing we did was to tell the woman who had looked after them to go home, and to forget that she had ever worked there. We gave her the little food that was there as an incentive to keep quiet. We then went through all the men's belongings, to see if there was anything of value to the resistance. Other than a few pocket knives and watches, there was nothing we could use. The men's clothing we distributed to some of the poorer people in the village, refugees from Paris that had fled here during the invasion."

I asked again, impatient to find out. "Were there any papers? Any letters or other documents that might identify who the men were?"

M. Daniel shook his head. "No, nothing like that. There were a few photographs, though. I had no idea what to do with them – the Germans certainly wouldn't be interested in them and there was no way of contacting anyone else. I put them in an old tobacco tin and put it in my desk. I haven't seen it since then, but I assume it is still there. Would you like to see them?"

"Yes, please!" I almost shouted.

M. Daniel took what remained of his sandwich, wrapped it deftly with his one hand in a paper napkin, and put it in his jacket pocket. He got up, slowly but steadily, took his beret from the back of his chair and started for the door. I went to pay for the drinks and sandwiches, and Jack accompanied him. I caught up with them outside and we all walked left along the sea wall, and then turned into a small alley. At one of the smaller houses M.

Daniel stopped, pulled an old iron key out of his left trouser pocket and unlocked the wooden door. Without looking back to see if we were still there, he entered the house and started climbing the narrow stairs.

After two flights of stairs, we reached what was obviously the attic, with a steeply slanted roof. The old man pushed open the door and went inside. We followed, not knowing exactly what to expect. Inside was a compact one-room apartment, like what the British call a "bed-sitter". An old single bed stood on one side, neatly made and covered with what looked strangely like an Israeli embroidered bedspread. On the other there was a small kitchen table, gas-ring and tiny refrigerator. In between was a pair of old easy-chairs, and a bookcase-cum-desk, with a small radio-tape recorder on the top. Every inch of remaining space had cupboards of various shapes and sizes, and as a result, the place was spotless and neat, with nothing at all lying around. It was all 'ship-shape'.

Monsieur Daniel placed his beret on a hook on the back of the door, and went directly to the desk. Opening one of the drawers, he groped around in the back for a few seconds and then withdrew his arm, holding an old and rusty tin can. He gave it to me, and sat down on a chair by the kitchen table. "Sit down, *mes amis*, and have a look."

I grabbed the tin from him – impolite, but I couldn't control myself – and started to go through the photographs. There were an even dozen of them, they were all small, none bigger than 4 x 6 cms, and in black and white of course. Many were faded, and most were damaged in one way or another. I went through them slowly, impatient and yet fearful of what I might find. In the end, what I did find was beyond my wildest expectations.

I sat stunned, speechless, and my heart raced. Jack looked at me, and said: "You OK Sammy? You're as white as a sheet."

I couldn't answer him, I couldn't speak. After a minute or two, I slowly reached into my backpack and pulled out the little Perspex frame my father had given me. I laid it on the table, and next to it, one of the photographs from the tin. I didn't say a word, just pointed at the two pictures.

Jack picked up the frame, and then the little faded sepia photograph. He looked back and forth at the two of them, and then looked at me with his mouth hanging open. "It can't be!" he mumbled. "It's too weird to be true." I looked back at him and just nodded, still numb.

M. Daniel had a blank look on his face, since we were talking English between ourselves and he could not understand what we were saying. "*Qu'est-ce qu'il y a?*" I just pushed the two pictures over to his side of the table, switched back into French, and said "*Regardez*" - Have a look.

He picked them up and looked at them closely. "But how is this possible? Who are these people and why do you have this picture?"

"These are my grandfather, my grand-uncle, and Jack's grandfather. My grand-uncle disappeared during the war, and I have been researching what happened to him. It appears that by a complete and very strange coincidence, he was one of the athletes that were in that tunnel, and that were killed by the bomb. You have solved a sixty-year old mystery, and brought peace of mind to myself, and my father."

"*Incroyable!*" Unbelievable, he said. "I am so glad that I saved those photographs all these years, and was able to help you. But you are wrong on one account. The man in the photograph was not killed by the bomb. It was he who fought with the German Captain and killed him, dying in the process. So you can be very, very proud of your Grand-uncle. And I can do one more thing for you. Are you going to the Mont now?"

"Well, we can." said Jack. "We have no firm plans, so it is no problem."

"Well, if you can take me along, I will show you something there that will help you more. And don't worry about bringing me back here. I have friends in the village that I have not seen for several months, and I will go stay with them. Let me just call them to be sure."

A short phone call produced the desired invitation for M. Daniel to come and stay with his friends, and we left. Thankfully, we had rented a real car for this trip – I would not have wanted

M. Daniel to suffer the indignities of riding in (or on) Gertrude the Jeep.

# Chapter XX

On the way to Mont St. Michel M. Daniel sat quietly in the back seat, sunk in thought about people and events that were long past. Jack and I discussed the events of the afternoon, and how we would break the news to our parents.

On arrival at the Mont, M. Daniel directed us to the back side of the village – the side facing the English Channel. Below the abbey was the local cemetery, and once we were in it, he led us to the back wall where there was a small gate, rusted and overgrown with vines and weeds. M. Daniel motioned to us to open the gate, which was not an easy task, as the vegetation was thick and the gate resisted.

Jack reached into his pocket and pulled out a Swiss Army Knife. "Always have one of these on me, you never know when you are going to need one." Using the knife, he cut away the vines while I pulled at the gate. After a few minutes' work the gate was freed. I pulled it open far enough so that we could get through and the three of us left the main cemetery area. Outside the wall, partially hidden by the wild growth, were ten tombstones. M. Daniel pushed through the vegetation, reached one of the gravestones and started rubbing the surface. "Voila" he said, "This is what I wanted you to see."

Engraved on the tombstone, and barely visible after all these years was a *Magen David* – The Star of David.

"We didn't have names for the men who were killed, but we knew they were Jewish. The church wouldn't let us bury them inside the cemetery, but there was this little plot outside the walls, and they allowed us to bury them there. We put numbers on them, to identify them, and I made marks on the backs of the photographs we found. Your great uncle was number One, as he was the one who fought with the German. This is his gravestone."

I was speechless, dumbfounded and in shock. The circle was closed, the mystery solved, and now the grave – complete closure. I shook my head, looked at Jack who was also stunned, and said to M. Daniel: "Merci M. Daniel. You have done a wonderful thing, and my family will be eternally grateful."

I continued: "But there are ten tombstones here, We know that there were twelve prisoners originally – do you know anything about the other two?

"*Pardon*, I forgot. Your granduncle, when he told me the story, also told me that two of the men had already died, as a result of their labors or accidents, it wasn't clear to me. When I asked him what had been done with their bodies, he just shrugged. What happened to people after they died was by that time no longer of interest to people in their position. So, I'm afraid I have no idea."

"That's alright M. Daniel. I was just curious, and hoping for a better outcome."

I pulled my slouch hat out of my pack, put it on my head, and began to recite the *Mourner's Kaddish* – the Jewish prayer for the dead: "*Yeetgadal v' yeetkadash sh'mey rabbah*". Jack joined in, stumbling and not knowing all the words, but doing his best, and M. Daniel did the same. We finished up, more or less together, and with all three of us managing to remember the last lines:

*Oseh shalom beem'roh'mahv, hoo ya'aseh shalom, aleynu v'al kohl yisrael v'eemru: Amen*

'He Who makes peace on high, may He make peace, upon us and upon all Israel, and let us now say: Amen.'

There wasn't a dry eye amongst us, and I felt an enormous sense of relief. Jack opened his pack, and pulled out his digital camera. He took pictures of all the gravestones we could find, and several of *Onkel* Samuel's, and the rest of the cemetery, the wall and the gate.

Closing the gate behind us, we went back to the village, dropped M. Daniel at his friends and headed for the causeway. Before we parted, I had some last questions for him. "M. Daniel, when we asked the waiter in the cafe here in the village if he knew anyone that could help us, he totally ignored us, but when we left, he came up to us in an alleyway and told us to come to St. Malo. Do you have any idea why he behaved so strangely?"

M. Daniel nodded. "Even today, some 60 years after the end of the war, people are still sensitive about certain subjects here.

There were people who behaved properly during the war, and there were others that didn't. People don't like talking about that time in general, and even less so in public. I guess he was just being careful."

"One more question, if you don't mind." I said.

"*S'ils vous plaît, mon ami.*"

"This has nothing really to do with this quest of ours, I just wanted to ask if by any chance you know anything about a German soldier – a translator, who disappeared in 1942. I don't even know if it was in this area, but since we have had so many coincidences, I thought I would try again. His name was Fritz Schmiltz, he would have been about 22 or 23 at the time."

M. Daniel leaned against the nearest house, to rest for a moment, and then said: "I have no idea what his name was, but there was a young German soldier who deserted from the Avranches garrison about that time. I did not know him well, though I met him once or twice. His ability to translate between French and German was very useful to the *Maquis* – the underground – and the local leaders kept him well hidden, since everyone knew what would happen to him if the Germans ever found him. In 1944, when the allied invasion took place, the underground decided that since he was a German soldier, despite his having helped our cause for almost two years, they should hand him over to the allied troops. The local *Maquis* leader delivered him to some Canadian soldiers who were involved in the battle for Falaise, which is about 140 kms from here. I don't know if this is the man you are asking about."

I looked at Jack, shrugged my shoulders and thanked M. Daniel again. He went into the house to visit his friends, and we drove off the island.

There was a small cafe on the mainland end of the causeway, with a reasonable internet connection, and a phone booth. I had the first turn at the phone, while Jack downloaded the pictures onto my laptop. I had to speak to my father, let him know what had transpired and ask him to gently tell Opa what we now knew. I knew that it would be a relief and heartbreak at the same time, but knowing that *Onkel* Samuel had a real grave would mean a lot to them.

The phone call was difficult emotionally and the line wasn't the best, but we got through it somehow. When I was done, we switched places, with Jack calling his family in Canada while I connected to the internet and sent the pictures to everyone in the family that I had an e-mail address for, with a short explanation of what we had found.

We drove back to St. Malo without M. Daniel, and went to the hotel. I needed time to digest all that I had found out, and think about the consequences. A longer call home was needed, so that I could speak at length with my parents.

My father had taken the news well – there had never been any doubt in his mind that Onkle Samuel was dead - but my grandfather had not. He had been grateful for the news, and was proud of the way his brother had died, but it had still been a shock and he was not feeling well. My father was proud of what I had accomplished, and my mother just wanted to know when I was coming home.

No one in the family even mentioned the idea of bringing the body of my uncle to Israel for burial. We had no real religious feelings about this, no need to inter him in so-called holy land, and felt that it was right that he would remain where he had fallen, doing his best to be free and dying in the attempt. Perhaps one day we would do something about the gravestone, but for now, we would let things be.

Two days later we were both on our ways back home. I stopped in Berlin for a day, just to pick up my things and make sure I hadn't left any bills unpaid. I also paid a visit to Hans Dieter von Marburg at the *Limburger Altersheim* to bring him up to date, and then headed for the airport. Jack had gone from St. Malo to Paris, and from there, straight to Montreal.

In addition to my small suitcase of personal items, I had the two duffel bags with Max's boxes. They weighed quite a bit, and the El-Al check-in clerk had obviously gotten up on the wrong side of the bed that morning, as he charged me overweight for both of them. When I got to the security check, I had a horrible few minutes of concern – how would I explain the two boxes with Wehrmacht insignia on them to the Israeli security personnel. My luck was with me, as when it was my turn to go through the check I recognized the guard – he was one of my artillery buddies! A few minutes of 'Hi Shmulik, what are you doing here?'', etc. and he waved me through without a second glance and without passing my bags through the scanner. I had never been so glad to see an army buddy in my life.

At Ben Gurion airport in Israel, my whole family was in the arrivals hall, waiting for me after I cleared customs. My mother couldn't wait to get me to her table, and had brought what seemed like a five course meal with her. It was good to be back home.

# Chapter XXI
## *The Photographs*

After settling back into my life in Jerusalem, and bringing my MA adviser up to date, I got to work. It was only September, classes would only start near the end of October, so I had plenty of time to work on my own things. Besides writing my thesis and working on the article that Jack and I had decided to write, I put aside some time for another project. The box of twelve photographs from M. Daniel's desk in St. Malo was now in my office safe. This was one more chapter that I felt I needed to write, one more piece of the puzzle. After scanning each picture at the highest resolution my office scanner would allow, I put the originals back in the safe, made three sets of good prints from the scans and started on the next stage my quest, as I had now begun to think of it. In addition, I scanned the Monk's Manuscript, in color, and put the original of that also into the safe. I felt I should really give it back to the Bodleian Library in Oxford, but not just yet.

My family monopolized my time for the first week I was back, I had to tell them everything that happened over the summer – several times, and they had many questions. Unfortunately, I didn't have answers for all of them, but I had hopes of finding them. I spent as much time as I could with my grandfather, as he was frail and had not taken the news about *Onkel* Samuel well. He was glad that he knew what had become of his brother, but the details of what had happened were difficult for him.

I needed to visit several institutions to help me in my quest – the first would be the *Yad V'Shem* Holocaust Museum in Jerusalem, and the second the Pierre Gildesgame Maccabi Museum in Ramat Gan. Then, perhaps the Diaspora Museum in Tel Aviv.

I also needed to get in touch with Israel Broadcasting. For over 60 years there has been a weekly radio program called *Hamador L'hipus Krovim* (the Department for Searching for Relatives) that assists people trying to find lost family members. It had started out as a department of the Jewish Agency, in 1944, to assist the thousands of displaced persons who were looking for their relatives who might possibly have survived the holocaust.

On the first free Sunday morning I had, I started with the radio program, as I knew someone who knew someone at Israel Radio. I needed to talk with the presenter of the program, and persuade him to use our 'item'. After going through a series of secretaries and PAs, I finally got to him. I told him the whole story, in a very condensed version, and then said: "We want to try and find relatives of the other 11 athletes. We have their pictures, but they have no names on them, and we have no way of knowing who they are. I'd like you to add an item to one of your broadcasts, saying something like this: "Anyone who had a relative, who was an exceptional athlete and living in Germany in 1937-1939, and has no trace of what happened to this person, is asked to contact the program presenter." I gave him my mobile phone number so that he could contact me if necessary. (I had splurged when I returned from Europe, used some of the money from the Dresdener Bank account and finally bought a mobile phone.) It wasn't the normal sort of request for the program, but I made a good case for it, and the presenter in the end agreed to make the announcement in the next weekly broadcast.

The next day, Monday, I paid a visit to *Yad V'Shem*. They have hundreds of thousands of photographs, but matching the ones I had to any of theirs was a daunting task. I had no illusions about the possibilities of success here, I was just 'casting my bread upon the waters', hoping that someone in their research departments might by some fluke of chance, recognize one of the men. I left a set of the photographs with the head of the photographic research department, gave him a short run-down of the story behind them, and left it at that.

I had higher expectations from the Maccabi Museum (located on the grounds of *Kfar HaMacabia*, or Maccabi Village, where the quadrennial Maccabi games were now held), since they dealt exclusively with Jewish sports history and were known to have a large collection of material concerning German Jewish sports clubs. On the Tuesday of that week, I met with Joshua Marcus - their chief archivist, gave him the story and a set of photographs. He was amazed by the story, and had never heard of anything remotely like it. There was no record in this museum, or in any other as far as he was aware of, of any 'special treatment' for Jewish Athletes, and he did not recall any other story of disappearing athletes.

The museum's major problem, like so many other museums, was budget – or lack of budget, and he had almost no staff. He did have some volunteers, some of whom were foreign students that were studying in Israel, and he offered to put one of them on the search.

"That would be wonderful" I said. "How will they do it?"

"They can put your photograph on a split screen, enlarge the face of one of the men, and then run some facial recognition software through our collection of German athletes from the 1930s."

"Isn't that sort of software really expensive, and only used by governments looking for terrorists?"

"Yes, but ... one of our donors, who wishes to remain anonymous, has donated a *beta* version of a new program his company is developing. In return for our trying it out on various projects – like yours – he gets valuable feedback concerning bugs in the program, improvements we suggest, etc."

"What a lucky break – for you and for me."

"Yes, we thought so too. It works very well, but tends to break down when the resolution of the photograph is too low – or too high. I'm a bit worried about that with your pictures, as the originals were so small. What resolution did you scan it at?"

"The best I had on my office printer/scanner – 600 dpi."

"Hmm" said Joshua. "That's about the bottom limit – we usually try for at least 1200. Let me give it to my volunteer tomorrow when she comes in and see if she gets anything. If the program starts to complain about the resolution, you might want to bring in the originals and we can scan them here at a much higher quality – up to 4800 dpi. That scanner is another gift – otherwise, we'd be using off-the-shelf commercial hardware like yours."

"That sounds great" I said. "When do you think she'll be able to work on it?"

"Yael comes in twice a week – Mondays and Thursdays. She'll be in on Thursday, but will then be taking time off for the High Holidays. She doesn't have anything else on her desk that is really important, so hopefully she'll be able to start this Thursday. I'll give it to her to work on and then we'll have to hope for the best. As we have thousands of pictures, this will take a while. I'll have her start on the portraits we have, they are in a separate directory, as that is the most likely place where we might have success."

I gave him my card, with my contact details on it, so that he could get in touch on the off chance that they might actually find something, and left. On my way back to Jerusalem on the bus, I thought about all the possibilities and places to search, and remembered a letter I had written from Berlin to the librarian at the Wingate Institute.

After meeting and speaking with Frau Grenke in Berlin, at the beginning of my 'quest', I had written to the librarian at Wingate, asking her if she had any material on other Jewish athletes that might have remained in Berlin, or returned from the Maccabi Games together with Onkle Samuel. I never received any reply from her, and to be honest, I had forgotten totally about the letter. I made myself a note to follow up on this, and then leaned my head against the window and fell asleep. It wasn't a long ride – only about 50 minutes, but in 9 cases out of 10, I would fall asleep during it. Now, after my European holiday-cum-adventure, I was way overdrawn on my sleep and was catching up whenever and wherever I could.

- - - - - - - - -

I had returned just before the Jewish High Holidays, which together with the normally late start of the academic year in Israel, gave me some time to work on my materials before classes started. I managed to get through on the phone to the librarian at Wingate, and discovered the reason for the lack of reply to my letter. The librarian in charge had departed over the summer, without giving a reason or even a day's notice, and things had been chaotic ever since. A new librarian had started on the 1st of

September, and had never seen or even heard of my letter. Rather that try and explain the whole story over the phone, I made an appointment to see her on the 26th - just before the week-long Sukkoth holiday, when most institutions would be back at work after the summer vacation, but academic classes would not yet have started.

Family functions and visits kept me busy throughout the High Holidays, even though none of us attended the synagogue. Friends kept on dropping in, meals were huge and heavy, and in the end, I gave up and decided to take a break from the quest and just relax for a while. I really needed it after running around France and Germany all summer, with all the excitement that had occurred. There was no real rush to move forward.

So, on a clear and very hot September day, I took the bus to Tel Aviv from Jerusalem, and there changed to another one to Netanya. Five minutes before reaching this sea-side city, I rang the bell and the bus let me off at the stop for the Wingate Institute. A concrete footbridge got me across the coastal highway safely and I walked up the entrance road to the college gates. Wingate has a split-personality, being both an academic institution for training Phys-Ed teachers, and also a training institute for athletes of various sorts. It is also widely used by the military for getting soldiers into good shape. It is named after Brigadier Orde Wingate, a British officer with deep religious feelings and connections to the Plymouth Brethren. He had served in Palestine in the 1930s, decided that the Jews needed all the help he could give them and had organized the Special Night Squads, who were the spiritual and organizational ancestors of the early Israeli Special Forces.

I made my way to the Central Reference Library, located in the Pedagogical Center. Sarah Goldfarb, the new chief librarian, met me at the main desk and invited me back into her office. After a few minutes of small talk, I gave her the shortened version of my story, and came to the point of my visit. "Is there any material in the library concerning the athletes that came to the 1935 Maccabi Games, and that did return to Germany?"

She thought for a moment and then replied: "As I am still relatively new to this job, I cannot give you a 100% definitive answer. What I do know that we have are lists of the various national delegations, such as the Germans, the British, and so forth. As far as I am aware, there would not be a negative list – i.e. a list of those that did or did not return. What we do have, and which might be useful to your search, are individual photographs of the members of the various delegations. Each delegate, whether an athlete, or a coach, had to supply a passport photograph of themselves. This was used for identification purposes vis-a-vis the British authorities, as it was an open secret that the Maccabi Games were a golden opportunity to enter the country as a tourist, and then disappear into the general population."

My eyes lit up with the mention of the photographs, and I could barely wait to ask her "do you have the photographs of the German delegation?"

She smiled and said "Of course, and they are very well organized in albums. We are in the process of digitizing these collections, but have not yet started on the German one, so you can go through the albums by hand. Come, I'll show you where they are and let you get to work."

I had not expected such good luck, but had come prepared for every eventuality, which included a full set of the other eleven photographs.

There were two albums of photographs, of the type that immediately made me think of my grandparents and their photo albums from the 30s and 40s – pages of black construction paper, bound by a thick cord and a heavy cardboard cover front and back.The albums were divided into Volume One, with the athletes and Volume Two, with the coaches, medical staff and other ancillary members of the delegation. There had been 134 members, divided almost equally between athletes and others. So I had about 70 pictures to look at, and see if I could identify any of the eleven photographs I had. I probably should also check the second volume, in case one of the coaches had been in good enough shape to be part of Mad Max's group, but that would have lesser priority.

I took the first volume over to an empty table in the main reading room of the library, took out the first of the photographs from Mont St. Michel, and started going through the album. It was of a young man with dark, curly hair, but on the other hand, that more-or-less described most of the pictures. This wasn't going to be an easy task. I took the picture, and placed it next to the ones in the album, moving it around between the 5 or 6 pictures on each page, trying to find some similarity. Having had no success, I moved on to the next page, and repeated the process. What made it even more difficult was the fact that the pictures in the album were passport-style portraits, and the pictures from M. Daniel's box were, for the most part, family snaps. Some of them were en-face, and some were from the side, and in some you could barely make out the person's face. Some were of family groups, and some were obviously taken at some sporting event.

I had arrived at Wingate at 11 am, and by 2 pm, I had managed to go through the album three times, with three of the photographs, and had had no success. I had found a portrait of my grandfather, but that wasn't really progress, and it was a copy of a picture that hung in the living-room of our family apartment in Jerusalem.

I was hungry and disappointed, and needed a break, so I went looking for a place to eat on the campus. Leaving the album with the duty librarian, I went in search of lunch. It took me a while to find something, as I was totally unfamiliar with the campus layout, but in the end I found a stand selling sandwiches and soft drinks, which was really all I wanted. When I finished, I started back to the library and realized I had no idea where I was, and where I wanted to go. I walked over to the nearest building and went in, with the intention of asking someone how to get back to the library. It was a simple building, obviously used for classrooms and lectures, and in the lobby there was a collection of photographs on the wall, commemorating the First and Second Maccabi Games. Instinctively I went over to look at them, and within a few minutes, had found my Onkle Samuel, dressed in a singlet and shorts, standing in a chalk circle with a shot-putt in his hand. I actually knew the picture, it was one of several that my grandparents had of him, in an album they had put together with the few souvenirs and photographs that they had of him.

Even though I was familiar with the picture, it was still eerie seeing it enlarged, framed and on the wall. I went through the whole exhibition, looking to see if there was another picture of my uncle, but there were none.

On the second line of photographs, there was one which seemed familiar, but it wasn't of my uncle. I took out my pack of the 11 Mont St. Michel photographs and one of them was very similar to the picture on the wall. Under the picture there was a caption which read: "Ernst Goldblatt, Javelin, Maccabi HaTzair Hamburg, Second Maccabi Games 1935. I couldn't be sure that they were the same person, but there was a definite similarity. To cover all my bases, I took a photograph of the photograph on the wall with my mobile phone, even though I knew the quality would not be very high, and then found my way back to the library.

The album was waiting for me at the librarian's desk, where I had left it, and I went back to work. I went through it another two times, with two more of the 11 photographs, but with no luck. I was getting tired, and frustrated, and wanted to go home, so I took the album and went back to speak with Sarah Goldfarb.

"I have a couple of requests I would like to ask of you, if you don't mind," I said to her.

"Well, there is no harm in trying, the worst that can happen is that I'll say no," she said with a smile.

"Well, I happened to see an exhibition in one of the buildings here, about the first and second Maccabi games, and there was one photograph that is similar to one of my eleven from France. I took a picture of it with my mobile phone, but that won't be very good. The caption says his name was Ernst Goldblatt, and he was a javelin thrower at the second games. I'd like to know if I can get a proper copy of it, so that I can run it through the facial recognition software that they have at the Maccabi Museum."

"That shouldn't be a problem, as all the pictures in the exhibition are enlargements from pictures in our collection. And what else can I do for you?"

"I've had enough of looking at the album for today, and to tell you the truth, coming back here would be a real pain," I said, with true Israeli *chutzpah.* "Would there be any chance of scanning the pages in the album and sending me the scans by email? I don't mind paying for the work involved."

"That's a bit more difficult, but I imagine we can work something out. The picture of Ernst Goldblatt I can probably give you right now, we normally have extra copies of things like that. Let me have a look."

While she went looking through her files, I thought about what I was going to do next. I was impatient to have the picture of Ernst Goldblatt run through the facial recognition software at the Maccabi Museum, and I didn't fancy the idea of going back to Jerusalem tonight and then coming back in the morning, so I called my sister Naomi to see if she was at home, and if I could 'crash' on her sofa tonight. She was, and I was welcome, and the sofa was available, so I was all set. Her schedule as a medical student was at times overwhelming, but I had caught her on a 'reasonable' day.

Sarah closed her file drawer and handed me a copy of the Goldblatt photograph. "Here you are, and you don't have to return it. Just let me know the results of your search." It seemed that everyone I talked to about this project of mine wanted to hear the results! I thanked her for her help and for the picture, and walked down the hill to the highway where the bus-stop was. In less than an hour, after changing buses at the Arlozoroff Street bus terminal, I was at Naomi's place just off Nordau Boulevard – one of the greener and quieter streets in north Tel Aviv, having a quick beer before dinner.

I was always happy to see her, and we spent a pleasant evening together. We were only a year and a half apart in age, and had grown up almost as twins. When young, we had been inseparable, but the years had drawn us each of us in his/her own direction. Of course I had to tell her the latest developments about the photographs, and she was as excited as I was, if not more! My quest had been alien to her at the beginning, as she had not had the linkage to *Onkel* Samuel and the world of sports. But as the story unfolded and progressed, she had become a big 'fan' and had followed each and every development with great excitement. Her couch was less than luxurious, but was good

enough for the occasional night and I was up and out at 9am –
even before Naomi was.

# Chapter XXII

At the Maccabi Museum I found Joshua with a cup of coffee in one hand and a telephone in the other. He greeted me like an old friend, though we had only met the one time, while still on the phone, and pointed to a table where a young woman was sitting with her back to me, facing a large computer screen. My very non-Israeli manners kept me from saying anything to her until he got off the phone and came over to introduce us. When she turned around, she smiled with recognition, and I let out an uncontrolled "hey".

Yael Berkowitch had been in some of my first year classes at Hebrew University, we had been friends, and had dated some, but it never developed into anything and our paths had parted. I was delighted to see her, and from the smile on her face she seemed to feel the same way. "It's been ages," I said. "What have you been doing? And where?"

"Well, for now, I'm here. Let's catch up." Joshua looked startled at the conversation, but realized quickly that introductions were not necessary, so went back to his office with a quick "I see that I'm not needed here, so catch up and then you can let Yael work on your pictures – at least for today." I nodded a quick 'thanks' and Yael said "follow me to the coffee."

Over some stale biscuits from her desk, I gave her the quick, condensed version of my story, and promised to give her the full, unabridged version if she would have dinner with me. That came out totally spontaneously, and I had no idea if she would accept, or even if she was still single.

To my delight, she said yes, and I blushed slightly and asked her what she had been doing since I last saw her. When I had last seen her, she had been on a one-year program at HUJI, and had not had any plans to stay in Israel as far as I knew. "When you stopped calling, I decided to look elsewhere, and went back to New York to finish my BA."

I protested that I had not been the one that stopped calling, but it didn't seem to make any impression on her, or any difference.

"You can't do much with a BA in History of the Middle East, or for that matter, with a BA or BSc in anything at all these days. History had always been more of a hobby for me, rather than a professional path, and I had no desire to be an academic, so I went back to school for another two years and got a diploma in graphic arts. This was much more to my liking, and I specialized in photography. After finishing that, I worked a couple of jobs, had a few bad dates that never went anywhere, and got nostalgic for Israel, so I packed a bag and came back a few months ago. I have no idea what I'm going to do, and when I saw an ad that Josh placed looking for volunteers, I figured I had nothing to lose and it was better than doing nothing while I looked for something more permanent and more profitable."

"Lucky for me" I said. "This is the nicest thing that happened to me since I got back from Europe." I was sticking my neck out, again, but I figured I was on a roll. This time it was Yael that blushed and she seemed a bit at a loss for words. I saw that I needed to move on, so I pulled out the eleven photographs (the original 12, less the one of my *Onkel* Samuel) from M. Daniel, and the new one from Wingate, and said: "Since you have nothing better to do ..." and quickly ducked a crumpled piece of paper she threw in my direction. "Seriously, can you run these through the facial recognition software? Joshua seemed to be OK with it."

She smiled and said, "Sure, why not? Let me see what you have."

I explained that at this point, I wanted to compare the one picture of Ernst Goldblatt from Wingate against the eleven from France. In order to keep the process as unbiased and scientific as possible, I didn't want to run it just against the one I thought looked like him, but against all eleven – to see if the software would pick out the one I thought looked promising.

Yael took the eleven prints out of the first envelope, had a look at them under a magnifying glass and said "Don't hold your breath. These are not really as good as they should be, and the software gets annoyed when we run low-level pictures through it. I'll scan them at 2400 dpi, and hope for the best. If it doesn't like them, can you bring in the originals?"

"Sure, that's no problem. They're in my apartment in Jerusalem, so I can bring them tomorrow. First, let's see how it goes with these prints." She took the prints and put four of them on the glass of the flat-bed scanner. She then started the scanning software, and selected the pictures one by one. They were then scanned and appeared as numbered files on her computer. The process was repeated two more times, first with four more of the French photographs, and then again with the three remaining French photographs plus the one of Ernst Goldblatt from Wingate which I had given her when I saw how the process was coming to an end.

She collected all the prints and gave them back to me, and said: "Now the fun starts! This is really cool stuff, makes you feel like someone from the Mossad or the CIA, looking for a terrorist in an airport surveillance video."

The facial recognition software came up on the screen and I could see, even if I wasn't a computer geek, that this was a 'beta' version. It looked very basic, with no colors or graphics or anything fancy. Just two frames side-by-side. I must have looked skeptical, because Yael immediately said: "Don't let the appearance fool you. This is high-powered stuff and really good. The museum had to buy a new, fancy and very powerful computer just to use it – that was part of the deal. The developers haven't bothered with a fancy interface yet, they want to get it working perfectly before they spend time and money making it look nice."

She played around on the keyboard and the photograph of Ernst Goldblatt appeared in the right-hand frame. She then selected the other eleven files from a list, and typed in some commands. The pictures began appearing in the left-hand frame, one after another, and then again and again.

"Right now it is analyzing the faces from your 11 photographs, making notations and measurements of various features of the faces. This will not be easy, nor quick, as the faces aren't portraits, and most of them aren't *en-face* – looking at the camera. Once it's done with that, it will start comparing them with the twelfth picture. This will take a while; it's not a speedy process like they show on the TV cop shows. We can go for a coffee downstairs in the cafeteria and come back in half an hour, and I'm not sure it will be done."

"Fine with me," I said, and we left the computer to do its work without us. Coffee with Yael was fun, just as I remembered it had been a few years back. We fell back into an easy style of banter and chatter that just flowed and flowed. 'Why on earth had I stopped seeing her?' I thought to myself? Over the coffee (reasonable) and Danish pastry (awful), I gave her the full, unabridged version of the whole quest, and she just sat there and listened, at times with her jaw dropping. When I got to the part about the gravestones on Mont St. Michel, she was nearly in tears, as if it had been her grand-uncle that was buried there. She had always been a sentimental type; that was one of the things I liked about her.

We were almost done when Joshua came into the cafeteria, slightly out of breath and with a gleam in his eyes. "Come upstairs you two, we've got a hit!"

The two of us dropped what was left of the pastries without even looking where they fell, and I knocked over my chair in my haste to get up. The three of us ran up the stairs, tripping over one-another, each wanting to get to the computer first. When we got there, there were fireworks going off all over the screen and I couldn't see anything. "What the …?" I said.

"That's just a gag the programmers wrote into the software. It goes off when it gets a match." Yael hit the Esc key and the fireworks disappeared, leaving two photographs on the screen. On the right was Ernst Goldblatt, and on the left was one of the eleven pictures from M. Daniel's tin box. My instincts had been right, this was the picture I thought looked like him. And at the bottom of the screen was another box, showing the number 82.

"What does '82' mean?" I asked.

"That's the percentage of likelihood that the pictures are a match. In other words, there is an 82 percent chance that the two faces are the same."

"Wow! Success on the first attempt. This is fantastic."

Yael smiled at me and nodded. "That's pretty impressive, and a bit exciting, and to tell the truth, quite emotional."

"It certainly is. I'm a bit shaken by this, and by how easy it was. I'm sure it won't be so easy with the rest of the pictures, but this really gives me hope. Now I have to see if I can find any relatives of Ernst Goldblatt, and if there are, let them know what happened to him."

Joshua piped up: "I'm impressed. We've never had such a success, and so quick. If you want, we can go to our library and see if there are any records about Ernst Goldblatt, and if we have any information about his family."

"*Yalla*" I said. "Let's go. We're on a roll, maybe that will bring us good luck." But it was not to be. The Maccabi Museum had no information on Ernst Goldblatt, other than his name on the list of participating athletes from the German delegation to the Second Maccabi Games. I was feeling optimistic though, so I excused myself from the others for a few minutes, and called Sara at the Wingate Library to see if she had more information.

"Shalom, Shmuel," she said over the phone. "How can I help you?"

"Shalom, Sara. Sorry to bother you, but I wanted to know if by any chance you have information about any relatives of Ernst Goldblatt that are alive."

"I certainly don't know that off the top of my head." she said. "I'll have to have a look in our files. Why do you ask? Did you find a match?"

"Yes, we did. With an 82% chance that it is him. So I really want to find out if there are any relatives of his alive and if I can find them."

"That's wonderful news, but don't get your hopes up. We have very little information on the athletes themselves, and even less about their families. You might want to try Beit Hatfutsot."

*Beit Hatfutsot* is the Museum of the Jewish Diaspora, located on the campus of Tel Aviv University in Ramat Aviv, Tel Aviv, Israel. The museum traces the history of communities of the Jewish diaspora through the ages and throughout the world, telling the story of the Jewish people from the time of their expulsion from the Land of Israel 2,600 years ago to the present day.

"Brilliant!" I said. "I didn't think of that, but it certainly is worth trying. Thanks for the idea."

"You're very welcome. I'll let you know if I find anything, and please let me know if you find anything yourself."

"Will do. Hope to hear from you soon, bye." With that I hung up, and returned to Yael and the photographs.

"No luck?" Yael asked.

"Don't know yet, she has to check her files, but she said not to expect much. She did have a good idea, though," and I told her about Beit Hatfutsot.

"That's a really good idea, you know. You should be ashamed of yourself for not thinking of it yourself," she said, with a twinkle in her eye. The Yael that I had known a few years back was reappearing, in an improved version. This was going to be fun – I hoped!

"*Mea Culpa*" I said. "My bad. Trouble is that this whole business is getting out of hand. I need to check lots of places and I can't be in two or three places at once, nor do I have the time and energy to do it all. Want a job as my unpaid assistant?" I said, half joking, half in earnest.

"Double the offer and I might think about it." Yael said.

"Really?"

"Sure, why not. It might be fun, and even interesting. I only work here at the museum two days a week, so I have lots of free time, at least until I find a real job."

"Wow. This really IS my lucky day. If you're really willing to help, that will be fantastic." I felt like grabbing her and giving her a hug, but decided that it would be a bit premature. I didn't want to ruin the reborn relationship before it got anywhere, and I really did need the help.

In the meantime, Joshua had gone to his files, and he now came back. "Sorry, but there isn't anything useful about your Herr Goldblatt. The application for the games show him on the list of athletes coming, and also on the list of those going back – which was less than 10% of those that came."

"I'm not surprised," I said, "but if you could give me the list of those that went back, that might help in the search. And if there are any photographs of these athletes from the team, that would be fantastic."

"No problem. I'll photocopy the lists for you first of all, and then Yael can look for the photographs the next time she comes. That will make the comparisons on the software quicker, as there will be fewer faces to compare."

"Now we're getting some where. Shortening the list will make everything easier."

Joshua nodded and said: "Glad we could be of help. Keep me in the loop and let me know how you get on."

We shook hands and he went back to his office. By now it was past 2PM and I was hungry. I looked at Yael and said: "Lunch? My treat."

"Let me get my bag and I'll be with you in two minutes."

Two minutes turned into almost ten, but I didn't really notice. I walked out with Yael and we crossed the street, looking for a place to eat. Across the road there was a small strip mall and we quickly found a *Shwarma* Stand. *Shwarma* is the local name for this gastronomic delight, but it is native to all the countries in the region – one of the better results of the centuries of Ottoman rule over all the Middle East and the Balkans. In Turkey it is called *Donner Kebab*, in Greece - *Gyros*, etc. This was one of my real weaknesses – meat (usually turkey in Israel, and mainly lamb or pork in other countries) on a huge vertical skewer, broiled by gas burners on three sides, sliced off and then stuffed into a *pita* with a wide choice of condiments, and with some spicy or hot sauce on top of it all. I thought this was the height of Israeli cooking, but I guess I would learn better. In the mean time I took every opportunity to have one of these, and there were various varieties in different places. This one seemed fairly standard, so I ordered a full portion and Yael had a falafel. I covered mine up with loads of pickles, sauerkraut, fried eggplant slices and a *piquant* yellow sauce known as *Amba* – the Iraqi equivalent of chutney, and we grabbed a couple of seats at a table in the back.

We chatted about what we had done since we last met, and Yael pressed me for all the details about my quest. The part about the dig on Mont St. Michel particularly intrigued her and she wanted to hear more details about the manuscript. I couldn't tell her much, but I promised to bring her what I had the next time I came down from Jerusalem.

I had so many things to do now, and so many different angles to attack, that I didn't know where to start. I needed to check names at Beit Hatfutsot, and needed Yael to run all the other 10 photographs through the software, and I needed to check the list of the German athletes that *did* return to Germany after the games. I wondered what had driven them to return, just as I had wondered all these years why my *Onkel* Samuel had chosen to go back.

Yael really did want to help, and I was happy to accept for both practical and selfish reasons. After lunch we went back to her office in the Maccabi Museum and sat down at a vacant table. We discussed what needed doing, and who could do what. We decided that she would run the photographs through the software and see if there were any results – this would probably take most of her next day at the museum. Thankfully, Joshua was OK with this, especially as Yael was a volunteer and wasn't getting paid for what she did there.

I then remembered that the week-long Succoth holiday started on Thursday – most places would be closed, or open only half-days, for most of the next week. The museum would be on half-days, with Yael at work next Monday 'till 2pm only, so we made an appointment to meet at Beit Hatfutsot the coming Sunday at 9AM, to start searching their archives.

I would go to *Yad v'Shem* on Monday (if they were open) while she was at the museum, and if we didn't need to go back to *Beit Hatfutsot*, then on Tuesday we would meet in Tel Aviv to compare notes and plan the next steps.

I needed to go back to Jerusalem for the weekend – my mother wanted me home for the holiday-eve dinner and I had things to do as well. Yael walked me out to the bus-stop, and when I said good-bye, stood up on her tip-toes and gave me a peck on the cheek! By the time it registered on me, she was already on her way back to the museum, but things were definitely looking up.

# Chapter XXIII
## *Matchmaking*

Sunday's visit to *Beit Hatfutsot* was almost a complete washout. They had hundreds of thousands of pictures, and records of individuals and communities that no longer existed, but nothing in their system was capable of finding individual athletes, without having their names. I did manage to find a record of Ernst Goldblatt in their database, which showed that his great-nephew had filled out a form for him, sometime in the 1980s, which showed him missing from his home in Hamburg, Germany. The last contact with him had been in 1939. I wrote down the great-nephew's name and address, and put him on the list of things to do.

So other than lunch and a walk through the Tel Aviv University campus where the museum is located, we didn't really do much that day. Just being with Yael was fun – actually, more than fun, and I was beginning to have hopes and visions of where this relationship was going. Who knows?

Monday was Yael's day at the Maccabi Museum and I went up to Jerusalem to *Yad v'Shem*. Unfortunately, the situation there was more or less the same as at *Beit Hatfutsot* – loads of material, tons of data, but no way of putting it to good use. I found a copy of the same form for Ernst Goldblatt that I had seen in the Diaspora Museum the day before, but that didn't really help. I hadn't really expected more, but still, it was a disappointment. I finished early there, so I took a bus to the Central Bus Station in Jerusalem, and walked over to the Israel Broadcasting Building which was nearby. I found my way to the office of the radio program that searches for missing relatives, and luckily, the program presenter, Yaakov Hovav, was there.

"Shalom, shalom", he said. "I have a few responses for you!"

"That's great," I replied. "Can I see them?"

He handed me a brown, government-issue envelope, and inside were two dozen or so pages that were torn from a small spiral notebook, each with a message from someone who had heard the request on the radio and had replied to it. I sat down on a spare chair (without even asking) and went through them.

Several of the notes were from people who had no real connection to my search, they were looking for people they had lost in the war and were grasping at any straws they could find. I sympathized with them, my heart went out to them, but they had no connection to the quest. I put them to one side and asked Hovav if he could have a standard reply sent to them, that I had no information for them. He had a form letter for just such cases and said he would deal with them, and wished me luck with the rest.

What remained were some 15 replies, with names of the callers, and the names of their relatives that they thought and hoped might possibly be among the twelve athletes from the Mount. They had no way of knowing how many people we had found, or if there was any real chance that their relatives might be among them, but they had hopes. I understood them completely, and hoped that at least some of them would find closure from our findings.

I put the 15 replies back in the brown envelope, put it into my bag, and said good-bye and thanks to Hovav. On the way back to the Central Bus Station to catch a local bus to my Jerusalem apartment, I called Yael from my mobile phone and told her the results of my morning. Basically, it meant more work for her (and me), but it might possibly narrow the search and focus the work on a shorter list of people.

The next day I met up with Yael at the Maccabi Museum at 11AM. It wasn't her day to work there, but we didn't have any other place to sit and work, and Josh said he didn't mind, and she didn't have anything else planned. She had a large desk where we could spread out our papers, and try to work out a plan of action. I didn't want to spend a lot of time corresponding with the people what had contacted Israel Radio, as most of them would probably be dead ends. These people would all be desperate and emotional, and I didn't want to deal with that right now. It was probably selfish of me, but I just couldn't handle a lot of emotion after all that we had been through in France and Germany.

We threw some ideas back and forth, and by the time we had had lunch, it was late enough so that we could speak with Jack in Montreal via Skype. He was just getting up, and sleepy, but when he saw me and Yael on the screen together, he woke up quickly.

"Is that your new assistant, Sammy?" Jack managed to say before getting out of bed.

I had kept Jack up-to-date on my progress, and about Yael and her help, but this was the first time he had "met" her – so-to-speak. I made the formal introductions, and she actually blushed, which was cute. She was now a full member of our team, and it was right that Jack know her personally.

We gave him time for a cup of coffee and then went through our morning's deliberations with him, and told him what we thought was the best plan.

Jack was agreeable, and thought we had made the right choices, and we decided on a standard course of action. We – i.e. Yael and I - would send a letter (signed by me) to each of the 'radio responders', setting out in very general and vague terms what we had found – i.e. pictures of German athletes, who were apparently prisoners of the German Army – without going into details. We would enclose a release form, by which, if they signed it, they would commit themselves not to divulge any details of what we had found until such time as we gave them permission to do so, and not to have any claims on us for anything. This was to protect our academic interests, as Jack and I were preparing an article for an academic journal, and perhaps even two or three.

Once they had signed the form, we would send them copies of all the photographs that were still unidentified, and ask them if any of them looked like their lost relatives. If they did see a resemblance, we would ask them to send us back copies of any additional photos they had of their missing relative, and we would then run them through Josh's facial recognition software to see if we got a match. Any match over 50% we decided would be considered a success, and we would then inform the relatives, but they would be bound by the agreement not to disclose anything about this to anyone outside their immediate families, and especially not the media. We wanted to keep the "glory" of making an announcement about our findings and the missing people we had found, to ourselves.

We used the Maccabi Museum's technology to make up two sheets with all the 10 remaining photographs (the original 12, less *Onkel* Samuel and Ernst Goldblatt), and printed out 15 copies of them, just to be sure we had enough of them to go around. By the time we were done, it was getting late and Josh wanted to lock up. I didn't feel like going back to Jerusalem, so I called my sister Naomi to see what her plans were. She had a study group that was due to go on till 9 at least, but told me I was welcome to come and stay – but that there was no food at all in the apartment

"No problem, Naomi, we'll pick up a Pizza on the way."

"We?" Naomi always needed to know all the details of my private life, like any good sister.

"Yes, we," I replied, knowing what was coming.

"Is she pretty?"

I gave Yael a brief glance and said "Definitely".

"Great. It's about time. But be warned, that couch is not really meant for two."

"Behave yourself," I replied and hung up before she had the chance to ask any more embarrassing questions while Yael was standing next to me.

I turned to Yael and said "Sorry, I should have asked if you have plans for the evening, or if you even want to come to my sister's for Pizza and a bit more work. That wasn't polite of me."

Yael smiled sheepishly and said "You're forgiven, just because you're so polite and not like 99% of the other Israeli guys I've met. Must be that *Yecke* background. And yes, that's fine, I don't have plans, I love pizza and as long as you buy some beer to go with it, we're set."

We caught a bus to North Tel Aviv and got off on Ibn Gvirol Street, near to Naomi's apartment. It turned out that Yael had a room not far from there, on Pinkas street, so we stopped off there for 10 minutes so that she could change and leave some of her things there. She was sharing an apartment with two other girls she knew from her year at the university in Jerusalem, but there were only two bedrooms, so she was sleeping on the couch.

"It's not a great arrangement," she said when we got there, "and I really need to find something else, but until I get a paying job, I can't really afford it."

"You and a few thousand other young people in this country" I replied. "It's a huge problem, and one day it will come to a head and people will take to the streets to try and change it. Problem is, that Israelis are very set in their ways, and it is really, really hard to get them away from their TVs and out into the streets to protest something."

"Well, I sympathize, but my first priority is finding work, not protesting."

"See?" I said. "You're already a real Israeli." That earned me another punch on the shoulder and orders to pull a couple of beers out of the fridge, to take with us to Naomi's place. Five minutes later we were on our way out, with Yael spruced up and looking especially nice. Life was looking up!

Late September is still very warm in Tel Aviv, and at 6pm it was a pleasant walk over to Naomi's place. I had a key and let us in, as she wasn't back yet. We put the beers in the fridge to cool, ordered the largest size pizza we could find and waited for it to arrive. In the meantime, we spread out our papers and plans on the dining room table.

I made a file on my laptop of all the people that had contacted the radio program that we had not automatically eliminated, with their full names, addresses (where they had given them) and phone numbers. With Yael giving ideas and corrections, I typed up the letter we wanted to send them, and also the release form. It wasn't a really legal document, but I didn't want to go to the expense and bother of hiring a lawyer to do that, so we just searched for documents on the internet and did the best we could. It wasn't really critical, we just wanted to cover our backs as best we could. I plugged the laptop into Naomi's printer, and printed out copies of the letter (individualized for each person) and then copies of the release form. Each letter and form also got a copy of the two sheets of photographs, and they were clipped together. All we needed was envelopes, which we had forgotten to buy, but that wasn't a real problem. I'd buy them at the post office in the morning, address them, and then mail them off – and then just hope for the best.

The pizza arrived within the allotted twenty minutes, so we didn't get it for free, but it was hot and spicy. Together with the beers and Yael sharing it, it was the perfect dinner. Forgetting about the quest for once, we chatted about stuff and people we knew, and the space between us on the couch kept getting smaller. Naomi came in at nine fifteen p.m. and the space grew wider again. She smiled at Yael, after I made the introductions, winked at me, and went to change her clothes.

The rest of the evening we just chatted about this and that, and relaxed. Naomi's medical studies were really pressured, and she needed all the relaxation she could get. Close to midnight we all decided we had had enough. Naomi went to sleep and I, being the perfect gentleman, offered to walk Yael back to her apartment.

"You're a generation or two behind the times," she said, "but I appreciate the sentiment. I know how to get home and always have a small can of Mace in my bag."

"OK, but do me a favor and just give me a quick call to say you got home in one piece."

"Wow, you are a real worrywart. It's all of three blocks from here! Fine, I'll call you." With that she took her bag and went to the door. As I opened it for her, she again stood up on tiptoes and kissed me, but she missed the cheek this time.

I went back and cleared the dishes and the bottles, and made my bed on Naomi's couch. I was just about to go and brush my teeth when my cell phone rang – Yael had arrived safely. I got another good night kiss over the phone, and we both went to sleep.

# Chapter XXIV
## *Getting Some More Closure*

The next morning we went to the post office on Ibn Gvirol Street, and after standing in line for over half an hour, managed to buy envelopes and stamps for them. On a little tiny shelf on one side of the Post Office we put the letters and forms and photographs into their envelopes, sealed each one carefully and put the appropriate stamps on them. With a broad felt-tipped marker, I wrote "*Do Not Bend*" on each one, in Hebrew and in English. I managed to avoid standing in line for another half hour by catching the eye of the clerk that had sold me the envelopes and stamps, and just handed them to him. He threw them into a big canvas postal sack without even looking and we were done.

Yael wanted to see some friends, so I took the opportunity to return to Wingate and get copies of their album pages with the German Athletes. We made plans to meet again in the evening at Naomi's, since we had no other place in Tel Aviv that was 'ours'.

I found Sara in the library, and asked her if I could make photographs of the album pages with the German team applications. She had no problem with that, and I set to work. I first made photocopies of each of the album pages, as the pictures each had the name of the athlete under it. I then set up my digital camera on a tripod I had found at Naomi's place – I thought it belonged to some old boyfriend/photographer, who had left it there and never came back for it. The tripod was a good one, and was equipped with a spirit-level, so that the camera could be set up to be 100% level with the table top, with the lens pointing down. This way, I could copy the individual photographs of the athletes, at a quality that was almost as good as scanning them, and then I could download them at the Maccabi Museum and run them through the facial recognition software. It was a bit complicated, but it should work.

I spent most of the day there in the library, with just a short break at lunchtime for a sandwich and a soft-drink. By four in the afternoon I was exhausted, but I had a digital record of all the portraits of all the athletes from the German delegation to the

1935 games, plus photocopies of the album pages with the names. I called Yael at her place, she had just come back, so I asked if she wanted to meet me at Naomi's. The reply was: "What do you think?"

I blushed again, even though there was no one to see me, and told her I was leaving the library, and depending on the buses, would be at Naomi's around 5:30 or 6pm. If she got there before me, which was likely, she could wait at the coffee shop around the corner on Ibn Gvirol.

As I walked down the road to the bus stop, I saw one coming and ran to catch it. There is an old saying in Israel among young and foolish guys, that said there were two things you should never run after – buses and girls – and here I found myself running after both. So much for popular culture!

I got to Naomi's just in time to catch Yael leaving me a note on the door. I used my key to let us in, and called Naomi to see when she would be back. She said she would be very late, as she was studying with friends for a major exam in the morning. "Probably pulling an 'all-nighter'" she said, "so make yourselves at home." I hadn't mentioned anything about Yael being with me, but my clever sister had made the assumption.

I wasn't about to start cooking at Naomi's, knowing the normal bare state of her cupboard, so I asked Yael: "Pizza again, or Chinese, or Falafel?"

"Chinese, and preferably Szechuan." This girl was not only cute and fun, she also liked spicy food. Better and better! "I'd like to wash up a bit; do you think Naomi would have a spare towel I could use?"

"Sure, and I even know where she keeps them. Look under the sink in the bathroom, there should be some there."

While Yael showered (this was washing up a bit?) I ordered dinner from the Thai/Chinese place on the corner of Jabotinsky and Ibn Gvirol. Their prices were cheap, their portions were enormous and I was ravenous. Yael had proved that she could put away large quantities of food, despite her pixie size, so I ordered two full entrees and a couple of side dishes, plus two beers. That should keep us for the evening, and the delivery man arrived just as she came out of the shower

Over Szechuan Beef with eggplants and *Moo Goo Gai Pan*, I told her what I had done at the Wingate Library. I now had a folder of 74 portraits, with references to their names on the album pages. She was working at the Maccabi Museum tomorrow, and we decided she would try to use the facial recognition software on these pictures. I had brought the originals of the 11 photographs, so that she could re-scan them at higher quality.

"Cool!" I said, and that was the end of the business discussion for the evening. It had gotten late, and after I did the dishes (throwing the paper containers into the garbage), Yael suddenly said: "You know, I'm sleepy, and I don't feel like going back to that apartment. Does this couch open up?" I gulped a few times, looked really sheepish and said "Uh, I..., I think so. Only one way to find out."

It did, and that was that. Naomi never came back that night, and that was fine with us.

# Chapter XXV

On the way to the bus stop, I pulled Yael over at a convenient location and said to her: "Hey. Are you OK with everything that is happening? We haven't talked about anything at all, and this is all going very quickly."

She looked at me, stood up on tiptoes again and straightened out my slightly wild hair. "Of course, aren't you?"

"Duh, yeah" I said, in my coolest voice. "I'm just not used to such things happening to me."

She smiled and said: "If you hadn't been so engrossed with your books, you could have had all this a few years ago already! I knew way back then what I wanted."

"Yikes. Men are dumb, I guess."

"Yup. Now let's get moving and catch the bus. We have lots of work to do today."

I threw her a mock salute, said "Yes Sir, or rather, Yes Ma'am" and we ran for the bus.

Josh actually did have some other work he wanted her to do, but was kind enough to allow me to work with the software to see if I could come up with anything. He had promised to let me go through the list of the German Athletes, to see which ones had returned after the games, and true to his word, had already retrieved the list of the entire team, and of those that had returned.

I was given access to their files, and they were all either on micro-fiche or had already been scanned into their computer system. The German team was on their computers (thank God!) and I quickly found my way to their folder, under G:\Games\1935\teams\Germany\participants. What I now had to do was take the list of the team members that had returned to Germany after the games, and compare it with the photographs I had from the Wingate library. There was a theoretical possibility that someone from the German team had stayed in Palestine (as it was then) and returned to Germany later, before the start of the

Second World War, but it was unlikely in the extreme. For now, I would work with the lists I had.

Taking Josh's list of those athletes that had returned, I compared it to the photocopies of the album pages from Wingate, just to be sure that they were all there. There were only 12 of them, including my *Onkel* Samuel and Ernst Goldblatt. Strange that there were 12 names, and that I had received 12 photographs from M. Daniel.

I downloaded all the photographs I had taken at Wingate with the tripod into a new directory on the museum's computer (I had them on my laptop too, to be safe). It took me a while to find the 12 that matched the list, but when I had them all, I put them into a separate sub-directory to make my life a little bit easier, and set to work. One by one, I loaded them into the facial recognition software, and began to run them against the 10 remaining pictures from M. Daniel's tin box. They were already on the computer from when we had found Ernst Goldblatt, but I rescanned them now at 4800 dpi, so that the program would have a easier time with them.

This was now a slow process, as the remaining photographs from the box were not portraits, the faces were not always even looking at the camera and their original quality was not great. The program didn't have a lot of pictures to compare, but the points of reference were few and far between, and as I had set it a pretty wide range for comparisons, it would go over and over each picture, checking each eye and ear and nose and anything else it could find. I saw that it was going to take a few hours for the first one it was working on, so I left it to work alone (it didn't need me for anything) and went to look for Yael.

She was deeply engrossed in reading something and didn't hear me come up behind her. I put my hands on her shoulders from behind, and feeling really brave, gave her a small kiss on the back of her head and said "Hey you, how is it going?"

She turned around, and said *sotto voce*: "Finally, he's learning how to behave!" and gave me a proper kiss back. The rest of the people in the room started to clap and I turned bright red! I guess they all knew everything and were happy for her (and me) but I still felt embarrassed. My upbringing hadn't prepared me for modern girls, but I figured I better learn quickly.

Trying to look and act as cool as I could, I said to Yael: "The software is going to be busy on its own for several hours at least, so I came to see if there was anything I could do to help, or to steal you away for a coffee."

"Well, you can't read articles for me, the contents don't yet know how to flow from your brain to mine, so I guess coffee is it. Downstairs or across the street?"

"Across the street, definitely. Downstairs doesn't really count as coffee."

Over coffee and a sticky baklava, we discussed her morning's work (boring but useful for the museum) and the pictures that were running through the computer, and what we needed to do next. I needed to go back to Jerusalem at some time - staying at Naomi's was not a permanent solution for anything. We needed to wait for results from the mailing we had done, and hopefully we would get some results from the software that was running while we were drinking. We needed to somehow crank up the speed of time and get to next week, when we would hopefully have some answers.

"Are you able to take time off your job" I asked Yael. "You could come up to Jerusalem for a few days while we wait, and that way we could sleep on a proper bed."

"Wow, what a proposal that is!" This girl had a comeback for everything. It was lots of fun, but I needed to learn to be careful with what I said.

"Well?"

"Sure. They can't really fire me as they don't pay me anything, and Josh is really accommodating. Basically, he's happy for me to come in whenever I want. Everything I do for them is helpful and saves them manpower time and salaries. How long do you want to be up there?"

In Hebrew, going to Jerusalem is always 'up' and leaving it is always 'down'. It's factual, as the city is 900 meters above sea level, but it's also religious in the sense of being on a higher spiritual plane than anywhere else.

"Today is what ... Thursday? Let's say we go this afternoon, and spend the holiday weekend. If you're nice, we can have dinner with my parents – they think I'm an anti-social monk and I can prove them wrong for once! There won't be any mail at all till Sunday at the earliest, and we can spend some quality time together, see some stuff. How about you tell Josh you'll be back in the office on Wednesday? Does that sound OK to you or is it too much?

"Sounds fine with me, but meeting your parents is a bit scary. What if they don't like American girls poaching their son?

"Fat chance. They'll be thrilled, and I guarantee they'll love you from the minute they see you."

"OK, I'll risk it. Let's give Josh the option of calling me back on Tuesday already, just in case there is some panic or emergency. Is that OK with you?"

"No problem at all. We can go up and down as often as we like, it really isn't a big trip."

"Certainly not on an American scale – my father commutes one and a half hours by car - each way, every day, and thinks it's a short trip!"

"Sounds like a nightmare. That's definitely not for me. Tel Aviv to Jerusalem is already stretching it, and not something I would like to do every day, even with improved public transportation."

I paid the bill (being the true gentleman) and we went back to the museum. Yael's desk had become more cluttered in the time we were away, with new files and documents that needed reading and classifying, so I went back to the computer room and the facial recognition software. As I walked in, the fireworks went off again, and I quickly sat down to see what it had found. It had matched one of M. Daniel's photographs (#6 on my list) - that of a young man in running gear and curly hair who was looking sideways at the camera, to one of the team photographs, and the box showed the number 67. Sixty-seven percent was not a great match, but in my position, I wasn't about to be fussy. I looked up the name on the print out of the file, and saw that the name on the form was Jacob Mittleman, and he was listed as a long-distance runner – 1000 meters, 2000 meters and 10,000 meters. This guy would have had stamina like nobody's business, just what Mad Max would have liked. On his application form he had listed a local relative, his uncle Menachem Mittleman. I guessed that if he was his uncle, and he had been around 25 in 1935, then the uncle would have been around 50 or 60 years old then. No chance he was alive now, he would have been way over the biblical limit of 120 years. But there was an address for Menachem Mittleman, in an old quiet area of central Tel Aviv, not far from the Carmel Market. I made some notes on the print-out, and put it into my laptop bag, and told the software to go back to work.

Back in Yael's room I found her bent over her desk, deep in concentration with headphones in her ears. Not wanting to scare her, I walked around to the other side of the desk and waved my hand just inside her field of vision. She caught the movement, sat up and took off the headphones.

"What's up?" she asked.

"We got another hit, though not as good a match as last time."

"Fantastic! How good was the match?"

"Only 67%, but I have a name, and the name of a local relative, so I want to see if we can trace him."

"Wonderful. I'm so pleased for you" and with that I got another smoochy kiss.

"I don't want to bother you, and I don't want to annoy Josh, so would you mind if I went back to Naomi's to do some phone calls? We can meet there after you are done, or at the bus terminal on Arlosoroff Street, and then go to Jerusalem?"

"Sure. Bus terminal sounds fine to me. I'll give you a call when I'm leaving here – there is a direct bus from across the street straight to Arlosoroff."

"It's a deal. Just don't forget to eat something at some time, because by the time we get to my place it will be late and there is next-to-nothing in the cupboard or the fridge and everything will be closed. Oh, and please turn off the Facial Recognition Software before you go. If there are any more hits, copy down the details on the appropriate form and bring it with you. OK?"

"Not to worry. Now go away and let me work."

I said a quick thanks and good-bye to Josh and left. The bus across the street took me to the center of Tel Aviv, and I wanted to see if by some freak of chance there were any Mittlemans still living at the address listed.

I managed to get a seat on the bus to Tel Aviv, so I made use of the time. Out of curiosity, I looked through the notes about the people who had contacted the radio program. I must have been born under a lucky star or some such thing, as there was a page with the name Yoav Mittleman, and he had given his address as Rehov Rashi 17, Tel Aviv – the same address as was on the form for Menachem Mittleman! I got a slight adrenalin rush, like when you think you are about to receive a prize, and tried to call the number on the paper, but the reception was terrible on the bus and I couldn't hear a thing. So I figured I had nothing to lose, and took the bus all the way into the center of the city, rather than getting off at Arlosoroff Street and walking to Naomi's.

There was a bus stop on King George Street, near the corner of Rashi Street, and I walked up the slight incline till I found number 17. It was an old and quite dilapidated building, much like the others on that street, but the area in the front was clean, and the stairwell at least didn't smell of urine – cat *or* human. I found the mailbox that said Mittleman, and the little piece of paper with the name looked like it hadn't been changed since the second Maccabi games in 1935. There was no indication as to which floor the apartment was on, so I just started climbing the stairs, looking at each door to see the name on it. Some had no names, and the stairwell light kept going out – an old eastern European piece of technology, meant to save electricity but probably the cause of many broken arms and legs as people tried to find their way in the dark to the next push-button to turn the light on again.

On the top floor – probably the fifth, though I had lost count by the time I got there – I found a bright red door with a ceramic tile on it that said, in Hebrew and in English, *Mittleman*. There was no electric push-button for a door bell, but there were some ceramic wind chimes that matched the name plate on the door, so I gave them a push and they rang pleasantly.

After a minute of silence, I pushed the chimes again, and then heard a voice saying *rak rega* (just a minute). I heard the key turning in the old lock on the door and it was opened by a young man, around my age. Feeling slightly anxious, I asked "Are you Yoav Mittleman?"

"Yes, that's me. And you are … ?"

"Sorry, my name is Shmulik Kaplan. You called the Department for Searching for Relatives radio program, in response to my request about missing German athletes from the second Maccabi Games."

"Right. Yes, I did. Come on in and excuse the mess."

I walked in and found an artist's studio – or more exactly, a ceramics studio. It was a bit messy, but looked exciting and smelled of artists' materials, which was nice.

"So, what can I do for you?" Yoav Mittleman asked.

"I'd like to ask you some questions, if you don't mind." He nodded, and I went on. "Does the name Menachem Mittleman mean anything to you?"

"Yes, that was my great-grandfather's name" he replied.

"Good. Now, do you know who Jacob Mittleman is?"

Now he began to get excited, or tense. "That is the name of my great-uncle, my grandfather's brother."

"OK, one more, if you don't mind." Again, he nodded, as if afraid to say anything. "Do you know what became of Jacob Mittleman?"

"No, I don't. He was a member of the German delegation to the second Maccabi Games and returned to Germany after they were over. We have no record of what became of him after that."

My head was spinning now, and my heartbeat was at dangerous levels. I pulled out the copy of photograph # 6 from M. Daniel's box, and showed it to him. "Does this look familiar to you?" I asked.

He looked at it and shook his head. "Is that Jacob Mittleman?"

"I think so. It has a 67% probability of being the same person as this portrait from the Maccabi games application in his name." I showed him the photocopy of the form with the picture.

"That one I recognize," he said. "I've seen that in family albums. Can you please tell me what this is all about?"

"Sure. Sorry to have sprung this on you like this." I then gave him a quick and simple version of my quest, and the story of the photographs from M. Daniel's box. When I was done, he sat quietly for a few minutes, just shaking his head. He then looked at me and said, "What now?"

"Well, do you know anything more about Jacob? Why he went back. Did anyone ever make any efforts to locate him after the war?"

Yoav replied slowly, choosing his words. "From what I know, and that isn't much, Jacob was an only child, and actually an orphan. When he came here to the games, he was 25 or 26, and knew no one here. My great-grandfather, his uncle, was the only relative he had, and there was no real connection between them. My great-grandfather was very religious and didn't approve of sports, Jacob only put his name on the form since he didn't have any other relatives here. I guess he didn't like what he saw when he came for the games, and so he went back to Germany."

"And your grandfather, his first cousin?"

"My grandfather had turned anti-religious, and had left home at an early age. He only found out about Jacob long after the games were over, when he tried to have a reconciliation with his father. That didn't work out very well, and they didn't talk again. When my great-grandfather died in 1947, my grandfather went through his papers and found out about Jacob and tried through the Red Cross to see if they could find him, but nothing came of it – there just wasn't enough information to even have a starting point for them. So the family gave up and we never really talked about it again. When my father heard the program on the radio, he called me and asked me to contact them and see what it was all about."

"Well, here's the information I have, the pictures and the form. They are all copies and you can keep them, and show them to your family if you want to. I wish I had better news for you, but at least you know the probable end of Jacob's story now – with a 67% degree of certainty."

Yoav shook my hand and said "Thank you for taking the time to see me. This is really quite an extraordinary story. Please let me know when it is all finished – you should write a book about it."

I smiled and said, "I might, you're not the first one to say that, but I need to find the answers to as many of the missing athletes as possible, so it may take a while. Here's my card, you can always reach me at that email address if you have any further questions. If by any chance your father or grandfather have some old photograph albums, maybe they can look and see if there is a copy of the photograph from M. Daniel's box – that would clinch the identity."

"I'll do that. Thanks again, and good luck!"

He walked down the stairs with me to the street, and I headed for the bus terminal. Yael phoned me while I was waiting to catch the bus, and we met up at the Arlosoroff Street terminal within minutes of arriving there. She had got there first, had bought two one-way tickets, and had a spot in a rather long line at the #480 bus stop – the express to Jerusalem. At that time of day, the buses filled up and left, rather than waiting for an exact timetable, and we only had to wait for two buses to fill up before we could board.

Snuggled into a double seat at the rear of the bus, we exchanged pleasantries until it left, and then once it was on the highway, I told Yael about Yoav Mittleman and his great-uncle Jacob.

"That's wonderful Shmulik," she said. "That's two down, only 9 more to go."

"Yup, which reminds me, I need to do some searching for Ernst Goldblatt's relatives."

"Well, you can look on the internet for them, but tomorrow and Shabbat are the weekend, and I intend to see that we spend it like a real weekend, and not working!"

"Deal!" I said, and got a kiss as a reward.

When I woke up in the morning, Yael was already dressed and making a sort of breakfast. The options were very limited - tea for me, coffee for her and some toast of questionable origins, with scrapings from the bottom of a jam jar. I made myself a mental note to ask Naomi to stock up on some basics – if we were going to continue using her place, I wanted to know that I could depend on more than a cup of tea. I wondered to myself what my sister lived on – maybe she was eating all her meals at the university? I put the couch back together, put the sheets in the hall closet, on 'my shelf' and we were set to go.

# Chapter XXVI

The apartment that Naomi and I had inherited from our grandparents was in the part of Jerusalem known as the German Colony, not far from the old train station. It had only two rooms, and really needed some fixing up, but it was dry and cool in the summer and warm in the winter, due to the very thick walls. The building only had four apartments in it, and mine was on the ground floor, which gave me access to the garden, which had grown wild from neglect. No one built buildings like this in Israel any more, land was too expensive and if a developer ever got his hands on all the four apartments in this one, he would tear the whole thing down, and build a tower with 30 or 40 apartments, no garden and no character. I was determined that this would never happen, at least as long as I owned the place, and thankfully the other residents felt the same.

My parents were thrilled to have Yael come to dinner, and scolded me for not bringing her around sooner. On Friday morning, after recovering from the holiday meal at my parent's house, I took some time and looked up the last name Goldblatt on the Bezeq phone company site. It depressed me, as there were almost 80 phone numbers listed around the country with that last name – and that didn't include those that might have Hebraicized their family name. I thought that the best thing would be to send a form letter to all of them, asking if they had any knowledge of a family member who fit our profile of a German athlete, who had taken part in the 1935 games and had returned to Germany.

Sending out 80 letters seemed to me insane, yet I didn't see a better solution. When I discussed it with Yael, her first reaction was "Wow, that will cost a bit. Can you afford it?"

The simple answer was, yes, and I explained it to her. My parents' bank account at the Dresdener Bank in Berlin was extremely well endowed and I had not spent much of it while running around France and Germany. My grandparents' pensions (from both sides), plus one-time large compensation payments for property confiscated, had added up to a large sum, which had earned interest for close to 50 years, and the total was currently over 100,000 Euro. It was a huge sum, almost obscene, and my time in Germany had barely scratched the contents. No one else in the family had ever touched it, and it was mine (and Naomi's) to use and do what whatever we wanted with it. Printing and sending 150 letters was peanuts in relation to the total in the account.

Yael looked at me and said: "Whoopee, I've got a millionaire in my clutches!"

"No, not a millionaire, but you've definitely got me in your clutches!" This time it was Yael that blushed.

After seeing the results of my search for people called Goldblatt, I had had enough of working, so we spent the rest of Friday walking around the city. I took Yael to some of my favorite spots, that she hadn't seen during her one-year stint as a foreign student. The one I liked best was the walk around the Old City of Jerusalem, on the top of the city walls, where you could see into the old city on one side, and over to the new parts on the other. Many of the city's best monuments and churches could be seen from this vantage point, and Yael clicked away constantly on her rather fancy digital SLR camera.

On Saturday 98% of Jewish West Jerusalem was closed due to the Sabbath, but the Old City bustled with tourists and locals alike, and we joined them in exploring the alleys and tunnels of the various quarters. Lunch was local falafel, with a snack beforehand of a typical Jerusalem bagel – huge and oval, and very soft, covered with sesame seeds – not at all like a New York or Montreal bagel, and served up with a small pile of *za'atar* wrapped in a twisted piece of old newspaper. Delicious!

Afterwards, we walked back to the apartment (it was only about a kilometer) and spent the rest of the day just lying around, enjoying each other's company and filling in little holes in what we knew about each other. I learned about growing up as a nice Jewish girl in the suburbs of New York and was amazed that Yael had turned out as well as she did – life there seemed to me to be totally divorced from reality – at least from what passed as reality here in Israel. In turn, I told Yael about my three years in the artillery, all the strange and sometimes nonsensical things that were part of military service in Israel, plus lots more details of the search for my *Onkel* Samuel and Mad Max's tunnel.

On Sunday we worked on the letters to the 79 Goldblatts, and made a trip to a local Office Depot store. I included my email address in the letter, in the hope that if someone did answer, they would reply electronically. Otherwise I'd be going back and forth from Jerusalem to Tel Aviv, just to check if there was mail. We stocked up on paper and envelopes, and a pile of ink cartridges for my printer. On the way back, I popped into the neighborhood post office and bought 200 stamps for local letters – I figured we would need all of them before we were done.

I had made an Excel file with all the names and addresses of the 79 Goldblatts, and I first produced labels for all of them, and then mail-merged the file with the letter I had composed. While the printer spat them out one-by-one, I signed and folded them, and Yael put them in to envelopes according to the labels on them, and put stamps on them.The Israeli Postal Service had gone modern and produced self-adhesive stamps for local letters – no more licking or using sponges to dampen the glue, which made our job easier. I stuffed the finished letters into the local red pillar-box (a remnant of the British Mandate and the Royal Mail) on the way to the supermarket – we had finished all the food there had been in the apartment and needed to buy supplies.

Monday I sent Yael back down to Tel Aviv, as Josh had called her and asked that she be at work on Tuesday after all. I spent the day working on my thesis, which had been totally neglected because of my search for the 11 athletes and my involvement with Yael. My advisor wanted to see me and get an update on my progress, so I went up to the campus on Mt. Scopus and spent a couple of hours with him. He knew the basics of my search, and really only wanted to know how it was progressing. Finishing the actual writing of the thesis would not be a problem for me once I had all the material, but as far as I was concerned, that would only be when we could identify all the 11 athletes. That might never be, but I was going to do my best and find as many as possible.

I spent the evening cleaning the apartment and arranging it the best I could, so that two people could live in it peacefully. I was deliriously happy with the way things were going with Yael, and wanted to do everything possible to make it work, and if that included cleaning and washing the floors, and making room in the closet for her clothes, well so be it. My night was unusually disturbed – I normally slept like a log, but this night was full of dreams about athletes running away from me and throwing photographs in the air – really weird. I was not used to dreams like this, but I could see where they were coming from – I was possessed by the idea of finding all the 11 athletes.

Tuesday morning I checked my emails, in the vain hope that some Goldblatt might have already received my letter and replied – foolish hopes, knowing the Israeli Postal Service, but I was really fixated on this new aspect of the quest. Having nothing more to do, I called Yael to see how things were at her end.

"Hi you! I was just about to call you," she said when she picked up my call.

"How did you know it was me?"

"Never heard of caller I.D.?"

"I've heard of it, but have no idea what it is or how it works. Remember, I'm a technological dinosaur."

"Well, if you're nice, I'll teach you all about it, and then you can screen my calls if you don't want to talk to me."

"Fat chance! I always want to talk with you."

"You know, you're sweet. I should have caught you long ago." She chuckled impishly.

"*Nu*, enough chatter, how are things at your end? Shall I come down today and crash at Naomi's? Will you have time to see me?"

"Good, yes, and yes. But first come here if you can. I have some things to show you, and that's why I was about to call you."

"So tell me now!"

"Nope, if I tell you, then you won't have to come and see me."

"You know, you're not as smart as you think you are – I'd come in any case!"

"Well, I'll take your word for it, but come down all the same."

"OK, I'll pack a bag and head for the bus station. I think there is some slow bus that stops not far from the museum on its way from Jerusalem to Tel Aviv. I'll let you know from underway if I catch it, and if not, how and when I'm coming."

"Fine. Miss you!"

Before I could answer, she had hung up. I threw a few changes of clothes into a small back-pack, grabbed my computer and put it into its bag, and headed out towards the central bus station. On the way out I check the mailbox on the wall of the entrance way to the building and there were a few pieces of mail in my box. I grabbed them and stuffed them into my laptop bag and left. On the way to the bus station, I tried to call Naomi to see if it was OK to crash at her place again, but the call went to voice mail, so I left her a message to call me back.

I missed the slow bus that stopped near the museum, but caught an express to the Arlosoroff Station, so it wouldn't take me much longer to get there anyhow. I had a window seat, which let me put my head against the glass, close my eyes and drop off within minutes of leaving the station – an old army trick that I had perfected – never lose the opportunity to sleep, even if it is only for a few minutes (or 45 in this case).

Less than two hours after leaving home, I walked into the museum and went upstairs to find Yael. I found her bent over her desk, with a large magnifying glass in front of her face, trying to read a faded and brittle piece of paper. After a quick kiss, she said: "Come with me and see your surprise."

She pulled me by the hand and almost ran to the room where the computer running the facial recognition software was located. With a few clicks of the mouse, she brought up a table, showing that four more of the photographs had been provisionally recognized.

"Wow! That's fantastic." I was overjoyed and slightly flabbergasted, as I had not expected so many more successes.

"Yes, and no." said Yael. "If you look at the fourth column of the table, you'll see that the percentages have droppped off. The best you got was 52, and the worst was 47. Below 45% it doesn't believe in success."

"Even so, this is amazing! We need to try and find relatives for these guys."

"Definitely. But it might be a good idea to check the names against the names of the people who called in as a result of the radio program. If there is a similar surname, then we can start with them."

"You're right. I'm so glad I have you helping me, and I mean that sincerely." That got another slight blush from her, which was all I needed to keep me going. "I think I need to build a table on a spreadsheet, to keep track of this stuff, otherwise I'm going to get lost."

I sat down at a vacant table in the room and pulled out my laptop. Opening up my spreadsheet program, I quickly set out a matrix like this:

| Picture # | Name (D for definite, P for presumed) | Likelihood Percentage | Confirmed by: |
|---|---|---|---|
| 1 | Onkel Samuel Kaplan (D) | 100% | Me |
| 2 | Ernst Goldblatt (D) | 82% | Wingate |
| 3 | | | |
| 4 | | | |
| 5 | | | |
| 6 | Jacob Mittleman (D) | 67% | Yoav Mittleman |
| 7 | | | |
| 8 | | | |
| 9 | | | |
| 10 | | | |
| 11 | | | |
| 12 | | | |

"So, let's see the photographs and the names that came up as matches."

Yael printed out the list the program had made, and I copied the new information into the table. It now looked like this:

| Picture # | Name (D for definite, P for presumed) | Likelihood Percentage | Confirmed by: |
|---|---|---|---|
| 1 | Onkel Samuel Kaplan (D) | 100% | Me |
| 2 | Ernst Goldblatt (D) | 82% | Wingate |
| 3 | | | |
| 4 | Shimon Schlessinger (P) | 52% | |
| 5 | Rafael Schwartz (P) | 52% | |
| 6 | Jacob Mittleman (D) | 67% | Yoav Mittleman |
| 7 | | | |
| 8 | Gideon Bernstein (P) | 47% | |
| 9 | | | |
| 10 | Benjamin Katzenstein (P) | 49% | |
| 11 | | | |
| 12 | | | |

"That's real progress," I said. "I probably should be ecstatic that we have achieved so much, in such a short time, but I really want to find all of these guys."

Yael gave me one of her looks and said: "You will, just be patient. You're doing amazingly well – you know that, don't you?"

I nodded and gave her a hug. I needed to clear my head from all the excitement, so after asking Josh if he didn't mind, I took Yael from her desk and we went for a walk through the Ramat Gan National Park, which is just around the corner from the museum.

We didn't say much for a while, just held hands really tightly and walked. When I found a vacant bench, I sat down and pulled Yael down next to me.

"What's wrong?" she asked?

"Nothing's wrong, it just that there is so much happening and so quickly, I need to calm down. I need to stop running around and back and forth from Jerusalem to Tel Aviv, and running to find you here at the museum when I need you or just want to tell you something. Am I making any sense?"

She gave me a puppy-dog look and said quietly: "Yes, I understand. It's fine, and whatever you want to do, I'll be OK with it. Understood?"

I nodded sheepishly and replied: "I hate being the 'alpha male', that's not my style, but would you be willing to drop the museum, and come stay with me in Jerusalem? I know you like it working here, but all the back and forth is driving me mad, and I'm pretty sure we can find you something to do in Jerusalem."

Yael nodded and said: "That's fine with me. We'll work something out, I understand how important this business is to you, and that you need a stable environment to work on it and try and come to some conclusions. I'll go tell Josh that I'm quitting, he'll be pissed but will probably understand. We can go up tonight if you want, or stay the night at Naomi's and go tomorrow. OK?"

I nodded back, and gave her a big, slobbery kiss and tight hug. This was my girl!

"Wonderful. You go tell Josh the bad news, and I'll try and reach Naomi, though it will be fine even if I don't get her. I'd rather spend the night at her place and go up to Jerusalem tomorrow."

Yael ran back to the museum, and I tried calling my sister. I got voice mail again, but that didn't really surprise me, as her medical studies were pretty intense. I left her a short message saying that we would be coming to stay the night and hoped that it was OK with her and didn't upset any plans she might have.

By the time I had walked back to the museum, Yael had told Josh, cleared out the few things she had in a drawer there and was ready to go. I made a point of thanking Josh for being understanding, it was always better to stay on good terms with people you have just hurt. As we walked out to the street, a cab pulled up to let someone out, and I waved my hand at him to wait. I figured it was a special occasion, so why not splurge on a taxi instead of taking a slow bus.

We spent most of the rest of the day at Naomi's place talking – mainly about how to proceed and what needed to be done, but also about us and where we might be going. Yael popped out for half an hour to talk to the girls in the apartment where she was nominally living. She was willing to keep on paying her small share of the rent for a few more months, just to be on the safe side, and so that she didn't have to start schlepping too many things up to Jerusalem. I would have offered to do that, from my German bank account, but I knew that she wouldn't accept that. Plenty of time for things like that later.

I needed to talk with some friends in Jerusalem about finding work for Yael, even if it were part time or free-lance, otherwise she would go nuts and end up resenting me, and I did NOT want that to happen. I made a few calls, and sent a few emails, and hoped that something would come of them, but for now I was happy for Yael to be unemployed, and with me while I worked on the project.

Naomi showed up around 6pm, tired and bitchy about her fellow students – apparently she felt that they weren't pulling their weight in the study group she belonged to. After a beer and a shower, and hearing what we had decided, she was in a better mood. We were all hungry, but the area where she lived didn't have any decent restaurants, so we reverted to Chinese take-away, and ordered it delivered, rather than walking the six blocks to the place and then back again. By the time it arrived, we were all mellow and in a good mood, and over the food we discussed what Yael and I were going to do.

"I wish I could help with some ideas about work for Yael" Naomi said, "but I don't know anyone in that field. Sorry guys."

"Never mind, we'll figure out something. Besides, I need a break right now, so that I can help Shmulik with his research or quest or whatever you want to call it. We'll be fine, once we're settled into the apartment in Jerusalem and work out a program for finishing this part of the project." Yael was really positive and up-beat about most things, which was one of her best characteristics, and it was a great foil to my rather pessimistic nature.

As we prepared for sleep, I pulled Naomi aside and said to her: "You know, you really should get yourself a better couch. You know you can afford it, so just do it. If you don't have time, I'm willing to order it for you on-line from IKEA and tell them to deliver it."

She nodded, and said: "You're right, I just need to do it. I won't dump that on you, I'll let a friend of mine take care of it, he complains about this one too. Hopefully by the time the two of you come to stay again, there will be a nice new and comfortable couch for you to sleep on."

"Thanks, Naomi. Lila Tov".

# Chapter XXVII

The next morning we stopped at Yael's place for her to pick up some things, and headed for Jerusalem. There had been no email messages for me from any of the Goldblatts, and I was worried that this particular picture would turn into a dead end. It was almost noon by the time we got to my place, having stopped on the way at the local mini-market to buy some basic foodstuff – *labeneh* cheese, eggs, milk, *pitot* and beer – the building blocks of nutrition!

When we got to my place, I unlocked the door, let Yael in with the groceries and then went back to the entrance to the building to check my mail box. There were the usual bits of junk mail and advertisements for things I had no use for, but there were also three plain white envelopes, the type people use to send real letters. I didn't recognize the names on the backs of the envelopes, but they were written by hand, so they seemed to be personal letters.

I gave one to Yael and said "See what this is about, OK?" and opened one myself. It was, as I had hoped, a reply from one of the people I had written back to from the radio station call-ins. It said, in short, that the writer believed that a relative of hers could be one of the 11 athletes. Her name was Berta Katzenstein, and she thought that her great-uncle Benjamin Katzenstein might be one of the 11. She had enclosed a poor quality copy of a photograph, but it was good enough to confirm that is was the same photograph as # 10, and that it was indeed Benjamin Katzenstein!

"Eureka" I shouted! "We have a winner!"

And then Yael piped up: "And another one!" I leaned over the table to see what she had, and saw a similar letter, again with a photocopy of a photograph. This time is was of # 5 – Raphael Schwartz. His great-great nephew had recognized the photograph as similar to one in a family album.

This was amazing, we now had positively identified six out of the original twelve photographs, including my uncle Samuel. I opened the third letter, and it was from an Oren Auerbach, who thought that one of the pictures - no. 12 - might be someone from his family, but he could not be sure. He wanted to check with some other family members and would get back to me. So that meant we had another possible identification. Seven out of twelve (including Onkle Samuel) was an incredible result, considering where I had started from. We had done really, really well!

I helped Yael unpack her things and made room for them on a shelf in my closet – we were becoming really domesticated. While Yael was in the shower, I called my mother and told her we were in town, and were going to come for dinner. Somehow, I don't think she minded.

# Chapter XXVIII
## *As Far as it Goes*

Between the High Holidays, the Succoth Holiday and all my running back and forth between Jerusalem and Tel Aviv, suddenly it was mid-October. Nights were becoming slightly longer, the temperatures were more reasonable – even cool at night up here in Jerusalem, at 900 meters – and classes were going to start at the university in two weeks' time. My MA advisor had arranged for me to teach an introductory course on *German Nationalism Between the World Wars*, which was really appropriate. I knew the material, since I had been the Teaching Assistant for the same course last year, but I still had to brush up on it. It was twice a week, at 7:30 AM, which was really cruel and unusual punishment, though I didn't know what I was being punished for.

Oren Auerbach had called to say that his grandfather had confirmed that the picture was Oren's great-grandmother's second cousin. His name was Kalman Tischler, he had been a sprinter in the Second Maccabi Games and had gone back to Germany to deal with his aging parents. From the time he left the games, no one from the family had ever heard from him again, but Oren's grandfather had a box of old family photographs and they had found a copy of the one we had. I asked Oren to fill out the non-disclosure form, thanked him for his efforts, and filled in another box on the Excel file.

I was pleased – no, thrilled – with the progress we had made, but there were holes in the table that might never be filled in, and that really bothered me. I had brought closure to my own family concerning *Onkel* Samuel, and to several others about their long-lost relatives, but I had a need to finish the job. Yael kept telling me on one hand that my expectations were unreasonable, and on the other hand, that I should not give up. Strange, feminine logic, but she was probably right on both counts.

I had started sending out reports on my progress to various people that had asked to be kept informed – Sara, the librarian at Wingate, Josh from the Maccabi Museum, Yaakov Hovav, the man from the radio program, the people who had recognized photographs of their relative, and various friends and family. They had all helped in one way or another, and certainly the least I could do was to let them know how I was getting on. In my last email to them all, I had included the up-to-date version of the Excel table, which now looked like this:

| Picture # | Name (D for definite, P for presumed) | Likelihood Percentage | Confirmed by: |
|---|---|---|---|
| 1 | Onkel Samuel Kaplan (D) | 100% | Me |
| 2 | Ernst Goldblatt (D) | 82% | Wingate |
| 3 | | | |
| 4 | Shimon Schlessinger (P) | 52% | |
| 5 | Rafael Schwartz (P) | 52%/100% | Great-great nephew |
| 6 | Jacob Mittleman (D) | 67%/100% | Yoav Mittleman |
| 7 | | | |
| 8 | Gideon Bernstein (P) | 47% | |
| 9 | | | |
| 10 | Benjamin Katzenstein (P) | 49% | Berta Katzenstein |
| 11 | | | |
| 12 | Kalman Tischler (D) | 100% | Oren Auerbach |

In addition to the fact that I had four photographs that I knew nothing about, I had two (Shimon Schlessinger & Gideon Bernstein) where their identities were based only on the facial recognition software, with very low percentages of a match. There was no real proof that these were the correct identities – just some computer software that thought it knew. I didn't know what to do about them, it bothered me and it cost me several sleepless nights.

After getting up one morning, I turned on the TV while I made breakfast – Yael was still asleep. The morning show on Channel 2 was interviewing someone about something – I didn't even catch what it was, but then, as the saying goes – "the penny dropped". I needed to get onto one of these shows, so that I could get some really broad exposure and see if I could find any relatives of these two athletes. I had no idea how to get invited onto one of the shows, but I was determined to figure it out!

The only person I even vaguely knew with any connection to the broadcasting industry was Yaakov Hovav, from the missing persons radio show. I had no idea whether he knew anyone from the TV shows, or had any TV connections at all, but *nothing ventured, nothing gained*. I had his phone number, so I tried calling him while the eggs were boiling.

The switchboard at Israel Broadcasting told me that Hovav wasn't in yet, so I left a message and went back to preparing breakfast. Yael was up by then, and when she had had her first cup of coffee and was more-or-less *compos-mentis*, I told her about my idea. She beamed and said: "Well done young man, that's a great idea. Now we just have to get you on all the morning shows so that the whole country will know about you."

"One show will be enough for now, if I manage. The thing about these shows is that not only do loads of people watch them, they tend to have an add-on effect, with newspapers and radio programs picking up the 'item' and spreading the word even more. So let's hope that Yaakov Hovav has some connections, 'cause I certainly don't."

Israel is a very small country, in many ways – some good, some really annoying. The most Israeli of these traits is that you can (almost) always find a connection to someone you meet. It's this 'six degrees of separation' thing – but much more intense and usually it only takes three or four degrees of separation to find the connection. A lot of this is due to army service, where you get thrown together with people from all over the country and all sorts of different backgrounds that you wouldn't necessarily run into otherwise. Using my network of old army buddies, I had found a graphic arts studio that wanted to hire Yael on a part-time basis.

Hovav called back between the toast and the second cup of coffee. After the usual pleasantries, I explained what I wanted, and asked if he had any good connections. Of course he did – this is Israel! A cousin of his has a cooking show on one of the commercial TV channels, and the cousin was well acquainted with the presenters of that channel's breakfast show. Yaakov promised to speak with him within the next few days to see what could be arranged.

I said to Yael: "You see, there are definite advantages to living here – you could never do this in New York or Los Angeles." I got a pat on the head for that, like a well behaved puppy, but I didn't mind. Yael went off to work and I stayed in the apartment to prepare for my classes.

Two weeks later, I got a call from the programming director of the breakfast show. I was amazed that she called, but managed to gather my wits quickly enough so I could tell her the bare minimum of what my story was, and what I wanted. She liked the idea, and told me she would get back to me soon. 'Soon' is really a relative term, it can mean ten minutes or two weeks, or never. I wasn't going to sit around all day waiting for her to call, but she did get back to me the next day. They wanted me to appear on the program the next Monday, at 8AM, which meant I had to be at the studios just outside of Jerusalem by 7AM, for make-up and preparations. An ungodly hour, but I was thrilled that they had taken the bait and invited me. Luckily Mondays I didn't have a class to teach.

Yael came with me, to give me courage and make sure I didn't run away – I really was nervous for my first television appearance, but I didn't embarrass myself too badly. I told a very, very condensed version of the quest, and showed the two photographs whose identities were based only on the facial recognition software, with very low percentages of a match. I gave the names we had come up with, and asked that if anyone knew anything about these two athletes, would they please get in touch with me. I also managed to get them to show the remaining four photographs where we had no identification at all. I didn't really think we would get any information about them, but there was no harm in trying. They put my mobile phone number on the screen, so that viewers could copy it if they wanted to get in touch. I was a bit worried about nut-cases copying down the number and inundating me with crank calls, but the producer assured me that this almost never happened. After thanking them for having me on the show, I returned home, Yael went to work at the studio, and we resumed our day-to-day lives.

A phone call a week later brought me back to the quest. A Giora Schlesinger had heard of my appearance on the TV breakfast show, but had not seen it himself. He thought perhaps that the photographs that had been identified as Shimon Schlesinger – the 52% match – might be a relative. He had a box of photographs and wanted to meet to show them to me. Of course I agreed, this was just what I had hoped for.

We agreed to meet at the Hebrew University cafeteria on Mt. Scopus the following Tuesday, when I would be on campus in any case. He would be wearing a Manchester United T-shirt (bright red, so easy to notice) and would be sitting by a window. I spotted him as soon as I walked in, and noticed the shoebox sitting on the table – presumably filled with family photographs.

We introduced ourselves, and I gave him a micro version of the quest, and showed him a copy of the photograph of the man we thought might be Shimon Schlesinger. He looked at it carefully, nodded several times, and then opened his shoebox. As I has suspected, it was full of old snapshots – by the look of them they were from the 1930s. He dug around in them for a minute and then pulled out a bunch of pictures wrapped together with a rubber band.

"When I heard about your appearance, I started looking through this box. There is a distant cousin of my grandfather's who disappeared during the war. Similar to your experiences, there is no record of what happened to him. Most of the family – those that lived in Hamburg, Germany – were shipped to the camps, but we have records of where they ended up. For this cousin – Shimon – we have no records. We think that these photographs are of Shimon, but there is no one left that can positively identify him. The other problem is that none of these photographs are the same picture as the one that you have."

I took the bunch of photographs from him and had a look. They were all of a young man, some in normal street clothes and some in athletic gear. I looked at the face, and at the face in the picture from M. Daniel's box, but I could not be sure they were the same person. The quality just wasn't good enough on both sides for me to be sure.

"I'm not an expert" I said, "but I can't be sure this is the same person. The only suggestion I can make, and what I would like to do, is to take your pictures and compare them to the one I have, using the Facial Recognition Software at the Maccabi Museum. That's how we got the name, and I think that is the only way we can come to any conclusion. I'm happy to take the pictures with me now, or if you prefer, you can have copies made or whatever you are comfortable with. I can even scan them on my office machine, here at the university – it's only a ten minute walk from here."

Giora thought for a minute and then said: "That sounds like a good idea. If we can go to your office now, and scan them, then I'll feel better – I would not want to lose these photographs."

"Sure, no problem, and I understand completely. Let's go."

Half an hour later we were done. I had scanned Giora's pictures (there were 9 of them in all) at the best resolution my office scanner could do – 2400 dpi, and I knew that this would be good enough for the Facial Recognition Software at the museum. I got him to sign the non-disclosure papers, just as a formality and told him I would let him know the results.

When Yael came home that night, I told her about my meeting at the university, and asked her to contact Josh at the museum, to ask for permission to come and run these new pictures through the software. After a short conversation with him, she came back with the OK – not that I had doubted that he would be OK with this, but it was good to be sure. We arranged to go down on Thursday already, as the computer there would be free and we would be able to work on the pictures without bothering anyone else. Yael told her boss at the studio that she needed a personal day off on Thursday, and that was that.

Everyone was happy to see Yael at the museum, and after a quick round of bad coffee and biscuits, we got to work. Yael scanned the nine pictures Giora had given me, and then pulled up our photograph No. 4 – the one with the 52% probability of a match with Shimon Schlessinger. She told the software to compare the nine new ones against No. 4, and we left it to work on its own. There was nothing for us to do there while it processed the pictures, so we went for a walk in the National Park next door again.

I always enjoyed the park, it has lots of open spaces and green lawns – I'm told it is like Kew Gardens in London, but I wouldn't know about that, never having been there. There is even a lake, and in the middle of the lake there is a building on stilts – in the early 'seventies' it had been a nightclub, but had closed for some reason and had never been reopened. Now it was just deserted and falling down, and the only ones using it were the ducks on the lake.

My life was good, I was stable and settled and had a lovely, delightful partner in Yael. Walking through the park, I thought to myself that I had been successful in my quest, my family had closure and I had done a good deed. Not bad at all. It would be wonderful if I could identify all the photographs from M. Daniels box, but we had done really well and what was meant to be, would be.

We spent a good hour walking through the park, hand in hand, like two young lovers (which we were). By the time we had finished a complete circuit of the park and were back at the entrance, my cell phone was ringing. Josh was calling us back.

Up on the second floor, the computer screen was showing its fireworks again, which was a good sign. Yael sat down and played with the keys, producing a list of the nine photographs we had run against the original one we had. The results were mixed, as was to be expected, but promising. The percentages ranged from 58% to 77%, which in my book was a success. We had found another missing athlete, and were able to bring closure to another family. It felt really, really good.

I called Giora as I had promised and told him the good news. He was quiet at the other end, and then said, as was to be expected: "I suppose that is good news, at least we now know what happened to this distant cousin. On the other hand, the story of how it all ended is pretty awful. In any event, thank you so much for doing this. I'm going to go visit my parents now and tell them the news. I hope they take it well."

There was nothing more for me to say to him, so I hung up and we gathered up our things to go home. Our table had not changed dramatically, we still had four complete unknowns and one – Gideon Bernstein – with a low probability. It now looked like this:

| Picture # | Name (D for definite, P for presumed) | Likelihood Percentage | Confirmed by: |
|---|---|---|---|
| 1 | Onkel Samuel Kaplan (D) | 100% | Me |
| 2 | Ernst Goldblatt (D) | 82% | Wingate |
| 3 | | | |
| 4 | Shimon Schlessinger (P) | 52%/77% | Giora Schlessinger's pictures |
| 5 | Rafael Schwartz (P) | 52%/100% | Great-great nephew |
| 6 | Jacob Mittleman (D) | 67%/100% | Yoav Mittleman |
| 7 | | | |
| 8 | Gideon Bernstein (P) | 47% | |
| 9 | | | |
| 10 | Benjamin Katzenstein (P) | 49% | Berta Katzenstein |
| 11 | | | |
| 12 | Kalman Tischler (D) | 100% | Oren Auerbach |

On the bus back to Jerusalem, we were both very silent. On the one hand, we had one more confirmation. On the other hand, we did not seem to have any prospects for identifying any more of the pictures. Maybe we would get another enquiry from my TV appearance, but so far there had been nothing, and the thought that we had reached the end of the road, without complete success, was depressing.

As we reached the bus station in Jerusalem, I had a thought. All the way home on the local bus I turned it around in my mind, but couldn't come to a decision. Once we were home, I sat Yael down at the kitchen table, and said: "Look, I think we have reached the end of the road here, as far as identifying any more of the photographs. Something we haven't thought about though, is what about people outside of Israel? Is there any reasonable, do-able way of getting these pictures publicized around the world? It's perfectly reasonable to think that the relatives of the remaining four are not here in Israel – we just never considered that possibility."

Yael smiled at me and said: "Oh, this fellow is so smart! I think you're right in thinking that it is a reasonable possibility. I just have no idea how to go about finding them. It would be a HUGE project, with no real prospects. Sorry to burst your balloon, but I don't think you can do it."

"You're right, of course, but it's maddening."

"One thing you might try though, is to use our connection with Josh to get your story told through the Maccabi World Union. There are thousands of people around the world that belong to it and I know they have an online newsletter, and a website, so if you could get your quest publicized there, and the pictures displayed, it *might* just get to a lot of people. People sign up for these things, but they don't always read them, so don't get your hopes up too high."

This girl was so clever, I didn't understand what she was doing with me, but I wasn't complaining! "That's a great idea, and I promise I won't go off the rails if nothing comes of it. You are definitely the best thing that has ever happened to me, you know that, don't you?"

Yael blushed her best blush, and I got a kiss – good deal!

I made her call Josh immediately, and listened in on the conversation. Of course he knew people in Maccabi World Union, and he would make some enquiries for us as soon as he could. But he agreed with Yael's opinion about what people do and don't read on the web. He said that he had placed ads for help in the newsletter, and had not received a single reply. "You have to be realistic about these things," was his given opinion.

So, we tried. Josh's connection gladly agreed to give me space in the next issue, which was two months away! How frustrating and nerve-wracking was that? We spent the rest of the evening trying to think of other ideas, other ways of trying to get the remaining four photographs identified, but nothing we came up with seemed even remotely likely to produce results. The odds were totally stacked against us, and it just didn't seem worth the effort to try.

I spent a restless night dreaming of photographs – all sorts of strange dreams with photographs stuck onto people where their faces should be. I woke up in a sweat in the early morning and couldn't get back to sleep. Yael was a heavy sleeper, and so my tossing and turning hadn't woken her.

I crept out of bed and went for walk while it was still cool outside. I hadn't done much exercise lately, so the walk was an effort, but I pushed and pushed and managed to do about 5 kms, up and down the main street in our neighborhood, before the shops and cafes opened up. I was exhausted and sweaty and puffing hard by the time I got back to the apartment, and found Yael still asleep – she could sleep through an invasion!

I had a quick shower to recover, made myself some coffee and toast and waited for her to wake up. When she had crawled out of bed and had a quick shower, she came into the kitchen and found me there, nursing my coffee and looking glum. "What's wrong, Shmulik? You look like you've lost a close friend."

"Sit down, and I'll tell you. I haven't lost a friend, but I've decided to let him go."

She gave me a 'what's wrong with him' type of look and said: "Huh?"

"I've come to the conclusion that I have to stop. The chances of finding any more answers, any more identities are so small as to be nil. Certainly unrealistic and highly improbable. I think I have to accept the fact that I will not be able to identify the last four photographs – ever. I have to let go. Can you live with that?"

"Of course I can. First of all, it's your decision, and it's your quest. Secondly, I'd come to the same conclusion a few days ago already, but I didn't want to be the one to suggest you stop – you would have hated me for that."

I gave her a hug and a kiss and another hug. "There are hundreds and thousands of people who disappeared during the war, in one way or another, and no one will ever know what became of them. These four will have to be part of that terrible statistic, and I will have to learn to live with that. Life is for the living, and we have our lives to live. So let's get on with it."

I got a thumbs up from Yael, I wrote a quick e-mail to Jack, and that was that. We were finished. Or so I thought ...

# Chapter XXIX
## *The Last Links*

Two years on, our lives continued. I had finished my master's thesis, and had successfully defended it. I was now officially Shmuel Kaplan, MA., and was now working on my PhD. Together with Jack, I was writing an article about the whole, strange story. We had already approached several academic journals and they all wanted to publish it – we just had to choose which one.

In an attempt at closing all the loose ends, I had sent Jack to try and find Canadian Army records for the Normandy invasion. There was a wealth of information on the fighting around Falaise, but he had not been able to find anything about Sister Beate's brother. His preliminary search had, however, been very perfunctory and we had not held out much hope for it.

We planned on working on this in the future, but right now neither of us had the time or energy to get into it. The size of the project was daunting – we had come to the conclusion that we might have to find the records for each and every unit of the Canadian Armed Forces that had fought in Normandy, go through them and see if there was any reference to this German prisoner. Another possibility was to somehow find the records of the 40-odd prisoner-of-war camps that had been established in Canada for German and Italian POWs. And we probably should interview surviving veterans of the invasion, though there were very few of them left. In the meantime, we had both collected a pile of books on the Canadian participation in the invasion, and were trying to read them one by one.

One thought I had, which I mentioned to Jack, was to try and put some sort of notice into some of the Canadian papers, and see if someone would react to the name of Fritz Schmiltz. It would be a difficult, and large, and probably expensive task, so we decided to leave it for now, but it might be the best way.

One day in May I received a call from Jack. His voice was a bit 'down' and he told me that his grandfather Nathan had died. He had been ill for many years with Alzheimer's disease, and had

had no idea of what was going on, but it was still a sad day for Jack and his family. We spoke for a while about family and history, and then hung up. I would not be going to the funeral, nor would anyone else from my immediate family – the distance was too great, the cost and effort too high. There had always been a saying in the family - 'Don't travel for funerals, use your money to visit people while they are still alive'.

Jack arrived in Israel a month later, for a visit that had already been planned in advance. Classes at the University were out, so I didn't have to teach, and we were planning to just have a good time together over the summer. Yael had found a full-time job in a small graphics studio not far from our apartment and was enjoying the work (but not her co-workers).

Jack took a cab from the airport and arrived at my place just after 5 PM. After getting settled into my spare room (it was nominally my sister's but she'd been living in Tel Aviv for several years already), Jack came to the living room holding a cardboard box and a plastic carrier bag from the Toronto Airport's Duty Free store. "Sammy, I didn't want to tell you this over the phone, I just didn't think I could do it."

"What is it Jack? What are you talking about?"

"When my grandfather died, we went through his things. We could have done it years ago, as he had no idea where he was or what was going on, but we didn't want to do it while he was still alive. After the funeral and the *shiva*, my father and I started going through his room and getting rid of tons of junk and old clothes. The clothes went to the Thrift Shop, and there were lots of books and papers, most of which went straight into the recycling bin."

He continued: "We did find his uniform from the Second World War. He had been in the Royal Canadian Air Force, but had never spoken about it all – not to me, nor to my father. On Remembrance Day, every year, he would get together with some friends from the war, but again, he never talked about that. When he became ill with Alzheimer's, he stopped going, and his friends didn't come to visit – guess they weren't in good shape either, or had already died. No one in the family even knew who these friends were – not even their names. By the badges on his uniform jacket, we figured out that he had been a Sergeant Pilot, in Bomber Command. I did some quick research through Wikipedia to see what all the ribbons and badges on the jacket meant. He had all sorts of decorations, and had flown over a hundred missions on the European Front, flying out of the UK."

"We've kept the uniform for now, not exactly sure what to do with it. Maybe we'll donate it to some museum. It was really strange, we had had no idea what he had done, and it turns out he was quite the soldier. There was a box with stuff from his RCAF time, his discharge papers and a bunch of commendations to go with his ribbons. And ... it was really strange, it was like a warped déjà-vu. After finding Mad Max's diary, we found my grandfather's wartime diary in this box."

I raised an eyebrow, as if to say 'you've got to be kidding', as I couldn't think of a proper reaction. All I could say was "And ...?"

Jack took a deep breath. He took the diary out of the box, and opened it to a place that he had marked with a little piece of paper. "Listen to this entry, dated November 27th, 1942:

> *Mission to the Rhine Valley. Takeoff at 03:00 hours. Bombs dropped over target, heavy flak. Aircraft damaged by flak, navigator badly hurt. Lost our way on the way back, flying by dead-reckoning. Found the English Channel after crossing all of France."*

By this time I was sweating and shaking, unsure and yet terrified by what was coming next. Yael was holding my hand so hard that it hurt.

Jack blew his nose on a tissue, picked up the diary and continued.

> *Aircraft lost altitude the whole way back, jettisoned everything we could. Found one bomb had stuck in the bomb-bay.*

*Bombardier loosened it, and as we passed the coast we released it. Managed to land at RAF Trebelzue in Cornwall."*

I was stunned. There was no doubt in my mind that this was the raid, and the bomb, that had collapsed the tunnel on Mont St. Michel. There was probably no way to prove this 100%, but I had no doubts and by the look on Jack's face, neither did he.

Jack was white as a ghost and trembling. "You know what this means, don't you? My grandfather probably killed his own brother - your great-uncle."

"*Shtuyot*! Rubbish!" I shouted at him. "Nathan freed *Onkel* Samuel and the others from Mad Max Vollendorf and the Nazi Final Solution. There was no way that they would have survived the war, not under those circumstances and not with Mad Max in charge. And it was Vollendorf who killed *Onkel* Samuel, not your grandfather. Nathan gave his brother and his comrades a chance, an opportunity to escape, to get out of the clutches of this nut-case. It was a lot more than six million other Jews had, and we should all be proud of what happened in that tunnel."

Jack looked at me with his teary blue eyes and asked: "Do you really think so?"

"Definitely. There is nothing to be sorry about, and I just wish we had been able to tell that to your grandfather Nathan. If I were a religious person, I'd say that Ethan and Nathan were now together in heaven, having a glass of wine and talking about old times. I'm not religious, but in any case, I would be proud of your grandfather, just as I am of my grand-uncle."

"Thanks, Sammy. I needed to hear that from you. Now, let's open this bottle of Canadian Club and toast his memory, while I tell you some good news."

The Canadian whiskey was not my favorite, but I didn't care. I got some glasses from the kitchen and Jack poured a generous portion into two of them. Yael indicated with two fingertips almost pressed together that she only wanted a symbolic drop in her glass. Whiskey was not her favorite drink – Bailey's Irish Cream was more her style.

"Woah there! I'm not a big drinker, and it isn't even dinner time."

Jack grinned and said "Never mind, you can nurse it for the rest of the evening. First of all, a toast to Grandpa Nathan."

"*L'Chaim*" I said, and then sheepishly added, "*To Life* is not exactly the toast for someone that just died, but it's always appropriate." We both took a generous drink from our glasses, grimaced slightly and then put them down.

"Agreed. And now for a piece of good news."

"I'm always ready for good news, though I prefer if it comes from the Lottery."

"Sorry, not that good, but still nice. In my free time, when I should be finishing my PhD dissertation and don't feel like it, I've been going through Canadian Army records – in particular, the histories of the units that fought in the Falaise battles. Remember that M. Daniel told us about the German deserter that the Maquis handed over to the Canadians?"

"Now that you mention it, I do remember, but I haven't thought about it in a long time."

"Well, it was nagging me and so I started digging. I like that part of doing research, it's writing the papers afterwards that I hate."

"Poor Jack!" I said and ducked as he threw a pillow at me. "So, tell me quick, what did you find out?"

"Well, this isn't 100% positive yet, but this is what I learned so far. The North Nova Scotia Highlanders (3rd Division) was one of the units involved in the fighting, which was fierce. In their regimental history, I found a reference to a German prisoner, who had been handed over to them by the Maquis."

Yael broke in. "So far, this sounds just like M. Daniel's story."

"Yup, and now it gets better. The regimental historian wrote that the prisoner's name was Fritz Schmitz, and that is almost the exact same name as Sister Beate's missing brother."

I quickly looked through my notes from the *Militärarchiv* in Freiburg that concerned General Schmiltz – Sister Beate's father. He had two children Fritz Georg (b. 1923) and Liesl Beatrix (Beate). "That's pretty close – Fritz Schmiltz vs Fritz Schmitz.

Can't expect much more from an army clerk in the height of battle."

Jack nodded in agreement. "That's what I thought. So whereas I never found anyone with the name of Schmiltz in all the major and minor databases I searched through, I never looked for a Schmitz."

"Nice work Jack. Did you get a chance to search for Schmitz?"

"No, not yet. That's on the top of my list when I get back to Montreal. I'm going to ask my research assistant at McGill to try and search the Canadian census, to see if there is or was a Fritz Schmitz. That will either eliminate the possibility, or bring us to another search, where I hope to be able to use a database from the Ministry of Citizenship and Immigration. In theory, they have records of everyone who ever immigrated to Canada. One additional hurdle is that Fritz Schmitz is probably a fairly common name, so there might be more than one of them in Canada."

"How can we be sure he stayed in Canada? Maybe he went back Germany?"

"Well, you did look for him in the German census records, without finding anything. He might have changed his name, or he might have died or been killed in the fighting, but we have no indications of anything like that. Many German prisoners-of-war stayed in Canada after the end of the war, so there is a good chance he did, too."

"So what do we do now about this?" I asked.

"Now? Nothing. It's a big project, and I'll start on it when I get back to Montreal, but for now, I think we're done here. If I get the time and funding to do a thorough search in Canada, that will be great, but there is a big IF there. Not really at the top of anyone's list of priorities, especially the way research funding is being cut in Canada."

Yael looked at me and said, "You know, we don't have a lot on our plates here, and I need to show you off to my parents in New York." I blushed a shade of beetroot red, and she continued. "Maybe we should go to New York for a few days and get that over with, and then spend a few weeks in Montreal doing that research. Rather than have your assistant do it, and waiting for your government to cough up the funding, this way we could keep it in the family – so to speak."

Now I really didn't know what to say, this was all a bit sudden, but thankfully Jack piped up with "That sounds like a great idea. We have plenty of room in the house, all my siblings have left the nest and the house is like a mausoleum."

Yael looked at me with a question in her eyes, as if to say 'what do you think?'

I look at her and said "Sounds like a good idea in principle, though I feel a bit like I'm being put on display." Now it was her turn to blush, which really suited her.

Jack disappeared diplomatically for a few minutes. I grabbed Yael's hand and sat her down on the couch. "Look, I know we've skirted this issue for quite a while, but what happened just now? Did you just propose to me?"

She looked sheepishly at me and said "I didn't really plan on it, but I think I did. Are you mad at me? Are you OK with it?"

"You always accuse me of being so conservative and formal, and now my girlfriend has proposed to me! What will the neighbors say?" She punched me on the arm, as she so often did, and said: "Well? I'm waiting."

"Nu, if you put it that way, yes. Of course I'm OK with it. I'm in love with it – and with you." That got me a big sloppy kiss and a hug and another kiss.

Jack came back into the room and said, "Everything OK? Did I miss anything?"

I said to Yael: "It was your idea, so you tell him."

She shook her head several times, so there was nothing else to do but tell Jack: "She proposed, and I accepted."

"*Mazal Tov*" cried Jack and gave us both a collective hug. "When do we leave for Canada?"

"Woah!" I said. "Not so fast. This just happened and we need to do some thinking and planning."

"Sorry" said Jack. "I got carried away in the heat of the moment. No rush at all, let me know what you two lovebirds decide."

"You'll know soon enough, but I think we need to speak to my parents first of all, then maybe it would be a good idea if Yael called her folks – don't you think?"

"Sounds like a plan. So go already *boychik*, speak to everyone and get it over with!" Jack had put on his idea of a Yiddish accent, which he used when he wanted to be funny.

We all went to my parents that evening for dinner, and while Jack diplomatically went for a short walk around the neighborhood, Yael and I told my family what we had decided. They were delighted – not only was I getting married, but they even liked my bride! Since none of us were in the least bit religious, and wanted nothing to do with the orthodox religious establishment in Israel, we decided to forgo a formal wedding in Israel, and just have a party for friends and family in a nice restaurant. Neither Yael nor I wanted a huge affair with hundreds of guests, and that was fine with everyone.

After a call to Yael's parents in New York (who took the news well – I think they had had suspicions that this was about to happen), we decided that after the party here in Jerusalem, the two of us would fly to the States. Yael would show me off to her family and friends, and then we would get formally married by a Reform Rabbi – Jack had a cousin in Calgary, Alberta, who was one and would gladly come and perform the ceremony. Again, it would be a small affair, just for close friends and immediate family, at her parents' house in suburban New York.

We saw no reason to wait, there was nothing keeping us in Jerusalem right now and I could work on my PhD thesis anywhere. So my mother got busy with making the arrangements (she was on cloud nine) and within two weeks it was all done. On the next Thursday evening, everyone showed up at the restaurant and ate more than they should. The party was nice, we actually enjoyed ourselves (which not all couples do at their weddings) and when it was all over and done, we considered ourselves married.

# Chapter XXX

Monday night we took the 1 a.m. flight to New York and Yael's parents actually met us when we landed at 6:30 a.m.! Greater love hath no man than to get to Kennedy Airport from Westchester at that hour! The Berkowitch's made me feel welcome from the first minute, which was a relief, and we had a wonderful pre-honeymoon week, spending most days in New York City. I had never been there, and Yael enjoyed showing me her favorite sites, like I had in Jerusalem. As a historian, I think the Cloisters Museum in upper Manhattan was the highlight of that tour – an amazing place. I could have spent a few days just there, but we didn't have time for that.

We both had a bit of jetlag, but it wasn't too bad, thanks to the Melatonin pills her father got us. The week went by quickly and on Sunday morning Yael got me into a suit (my first one ever!) and tie, and we tied the knot in the family garden. Jack had driven down from Montreal, so I had at least one family member at the ceremony. The rest of the day was a bit of a blur, people kept coming up to me and saying "Mazal Tov", but in the American inflection with the emphasis on the first syllable, instead of on the second the way it is in Hebrew. Sounded weird to me at first but by my third glass of Champagne, I wasn't noticing anymore. Yael was a beautiful bride, and kept me from drinking too much. Now it was official, we were Mr. & Mrs. Kaplan (though Yael threatened to call herself Berkowitch-Kaplan if I misbehaved).

Tuesday morning we packed our bags and put them into the trunk of Jack's car, and off we went. It was just over 500 kms from Yael's house to Jack's, so even with the stop at the border crossing for passport control, we made it in less than six hours. His parents were waiting for us when we arrived, and when I saw his father for the first time, I had a real shock! He looked like a twin brother of my father, who was his second cousin! Genes are really weird at times! We were tired from the trip, and after dinner went to bed early, but I couldn't sleep. I felt that I was close now to the last piece of the puzzle, and couldn't really wait to start working on it.

The smell of fresh coffee and bagels woke me in the morning. This was, after-all, Montreal, famous for its crooked, misshapen bagels – the cause of many, many arguments between New Yorkers and Montrealers, concerning which type of bagels are better. I didn't care, just helped myself to a large quantity of them, with Nova Scotia smoked salmon and local French-style cheese. If we stayed here too long I wouldn't fit into my pants much longer.

The plan was for the three of us to visit the McGill University library, and use its resources to try and locate Fritz Schmiltz or Schmitz or whatever he called himself now - if he was still alive, and if he was still in Canada. Jack's position as a PhD student at McGill got us into the library and access to their databases. We found a quiet corner where we could all sit at a big table and simultaneously work on our laptops. The plan was that first of all, we would try and find lists of prisoners at the 40 POW camps that had been set up across Canada during World War II. I hoped that the lists, if they existed, had been digitized, but there was no guarantee of that.

With the help of one of the librarians, we soon found out that there were no digitized lists – at least none that were available online, or in any of the local databases the university was connected to. Jack made a trip to the history department to consult with a colleague there who specialized in Canadian Military History.

After about half an hour he returned. "I've got bad news, and good news" he said on his return. "The bad news is that there are no digitized lists of the POWs – at all. The good news is that I have hardcopies for all the camps!"

Yael groaned at this news – she was not used to the pitfalls of academic research. I shrugged my shoulders and said: "Oh well, let's split the pile into three, and start looking. I just hope they are alphabetized."

They were, but not totally. Each camp had it's own system of listing the prisoners. Some had one complete list, some had them divided by years, some by barracks, and some seemed to have no system at all. There was no system as to how the prisoners were allocated to the various camps, or at least none that I could find. They were located all over Canada – from Alberta in the West, to Quebec and New Brunswick in the East. In all, more than 33,000 prisoners-of-war were interned in Canada during the war, and we might have to go through all of those names to try to find Fritz. And there was no guarantee we would find him. And, there might be more than one Fritz Schmitz. Let no one tell you that academic research was easy or glamorous – it was hard, and often dirty work. The papers with the lists of POWs were yellowed with age, brittle, and the files they were in were dusty to say the least.

Each of us took a pile of files and we spread out more around the table, giving ourselves room to work. I took the first file from my pile, opened it and had a look. It was from the Chatham, Ontario camp, and I saw that it had been opened in 1945. I said to the others: "I don't think there is much point in looking at camps that were opened only in 1945. If Fritz arrived in Canada, it would have been in 1944 I guess. That's when the battle of Falaise took place."

"Noted." said Jack, and Yael just nodded.

I went back to my second file, which was from the camp at Gravenhurst, Ontario. The lists inside the file started from 1940, and the last names were added in 1946 – long after the war had ended. How strange was that? I mentioned it to Jack, and he gave me a blank look, as if to say 'how on earth should I know?'

After thinking about it for a minute, he said "It doesn't seem to be relevant to our search, but if it ever does become a factor, I can always go back to my Military History colleague."

I made a note on my laptop about this and went back to the paper files. The Gravenhurst camp had had over 500 prisoners during the whole time it was open, and they were in two lists – one from the summer of 1940, when the camp was opened, and one from 1946, when it was closed. Thankfully they were both alphabetized, and I could quickly see that neither Fritz Schmitz nor Fritz Schmiltz were listed. On a hunch, I also looked to see if there were any prisoners listed with a last name of Fritz – such mistakes were known to happen, but there were none. I mentioned this possibility to Jack and Yael, who both nodded in acknowledgment and we all went back to our lists. The Gravenhurst file went onto the checked pile, and I took another file.

The Seebe camp in Alberta, also known as the Kananaskis Prisoner Of War camp (No. 130) had been a small one, with only some 200 prisoners. The list was short, alphabetized and clear, and our missing interpreter was not on it. On to the checked pile it went, and I took another one.

By 1 p.m. we were all hungry and slightly frustrated at not having had any results, though it really wasn't surprising. We left our files and laptops with a friendly librarian and went out for lunch. Vietnamese cuisine was the closest and we found a table for three while Jack went to get the food. Montrealers like to boast about the vast array of international cuisine that is available in their city, and Jack was determined to expose us to as many different types as possible. Vietnamese was a nice start – spicy, soupy and different from anything I had tried before. Yael enjoyed it immensely, she has a gusto for new food that is a joy to watch.

By 2:30 we were back at the library and into our piles of files. One by one they went onto the 'checked' pile and by 4:30 I had had enough for the day. "Enough already, tomorrow is another day."

Jack nodded in agreement and closed his laptop. Yael didn't say anything, she just held up her left hand with the forefinger extended, obviously trying to say 'hold-on' without losing her place on the page she was checking.

After another minute, she put her hand down, looked at us and said quietly, "I think we have a winner!"

Both Jack and I jumped up from our chairs and ran around the table to look at the file Yael was working on. It was from the POW camp at Farnham, Quebec - about 50 km ESE of Montreal, which had been open on-and-off from 1940 to 1946. There were three separate lists for the camp, for each of the three periods it had been open – 1940-1941, 1942-1943 and 1944-1946. In the third list, Yael had found a Fritz Schmitz, arrived on January 31st,

1945. He was listed as having been discharged – not transferred, on April 30th, 1945. This must be him!

I quickly had a photocopy made of the relevant parts of the file, and we packed up and left. We were all tempted to jump and shout with joy, but restrained ourselves until we were outside of the library. This really seemed to be our missing translator, the brother of Sister Beate. Now came more questions – why was he released before the end of the war, where did he go, and where was he now – if he was still alive. There were more questions, and each one led to additional queries – this was how research progressed, and why at times one lost sight of the original target.

The first question was a tough one – why was he released, and in April 1945? As a German POW, he should have been kept in a camp until the war was over and he could be repatriated. The camp file had no information about this, all it had was a list of prisoners, and a list of camp guards and other personnel. Finding any of them would be as difficult as finding Fritz himself, and many would presumably have died already of old age.

In a pub near the library, Jack, Yael and I discussed all these questions and debated how to proceed. On the really slim off-chance that there might be another Fritz Schmitz, we probably should continue check the lists of all the camps. We had done 21 out of the 40 camps we had files for, and that had taken most of a full day, with the three of us working on it. None of us wanted to be left doing that while the others went off on different tangents, so we agreed to return in the morning and finish them off.

Jack finished his beer and then got a look in his eyes. "You know, many of the German POWs stayed on in Canada after the war. Some of them hooked up with local girls during the time they were in the camps, and some just didn't want to return to Germany for one reason or another."

"How did they hook up with the girls?" Yael asked. "Weren't these prison camps?"

"Well, yes and no. You have to remember that this is Canada, and things are a lot more relaxed here. Many of the camps were very open, the prisoners would go out on work details during the day and return at night, with few or no guards to watch over them. Most of the camps were in remote locations and there was nowhere for them to go. There is a story told of a group of German prisoners that returned to the Ozada POW camp after escaping, having encountered a grizzly bear. Besides that, conditions in the camps were far better than what they could expect anywhere else. Some of them met local girls and some of them married them and stayed on."

"So?" I asked. "You think we should check the population registry or phone books or things like that around Farnham?"

Jack nodded. "I think that would be logical, and easy to do – either he's there, or he isn't. If he's there, or has family there, then Bingo! If he's not, then we look elsewhere."

"OK, that's a plan. Tomorrow we finish off the other files, no point in rushing things, and when we're done with those, we start checking the Farnham area for Fritz."

We had a quiet dinner at Jack's place, his mother was enjoying having him home, and with guests it was twice as much fun – she couldn't stop cooking. Reminded me of home, which was nice, and Yael was enjoying it too – her family didn't have the tradition of feeding people as if they were in dire need of nutrition.

The next day was a repeat of the previous one, hours in the Library with dusty files, and by the end of the day we knew that there was a) no Fritz Schmiltz in any of them, and b) there was no second Fritz Schmitz. We had located our man, now we 'just' had to find him physically.

Friday morning we were back at the McGill library, in a different room. They had a dedicated hall with dozens of computer terminals that were connected both to the regular internet, and to a massive number of public and private databases, libraries and government offices. We found three terminals that were free, next to each other, and started to work. We checked phone books (current and from previous years), social security records, tax records, etc. You name it, we looked at it if it was available. Using both names – Schmitz and Schmiltz – we combed the registries and searched the files. In the end, it was the most prosaic and the most predictable that finally produced results!

In the records of the Diocese of Farnham, there was an "*Eglise de Sainte Sabine*" – about 4 or 5 kilometers south of Farnham.

There, on the 15th of May, 1945, a wedding had taken place, between one Madeleine Fourchaud, 'a spinster of the parish' (i.e. she wasn't married) and Fritz Schmitz, a 'German national'. The bride had been given away by her father, Pierre Fourchaud, and the groom had been accompanied by Major John Templeton of the Royal Canadian Army! Curiouser and curiouser!

Jack had found this record, due to his French skills being better than mine (non-existant) and Yael's (basic American High School level, which was pretty poor). It was an amazing find, giving us location and some sort of justification for his release from the camp, but on the other hand, raised additional questions – starting with 'why was a Canadian Army Major standing up in church for a German POW?'

Next step was to see if he was alive. In Québec, the civil registers of births (baptisms), marriages and deaths (burials), which date from 1621, are duplicate copies of the church registers. A general index for marriages and deaths that occurred in the province of Quebec between 1926 and 1994 is available from the *Société de généalogie de Québec*, on CD-ROM. If we hadn't found the marriage in the diocesan records, we would have eventually found it there. A quick trip to the CD-ROM collection and we put it into Jack's terminal. A search of deaths using both Schmitz and Schmiltz came up with no results, which meant that up to 1994, our Fritz was alive.

I said to the others: "Look, we seem to have found our man. Whether he is alive or dead, and whether he can shed any further light onto the quest, I think we can only find out one way – by going to Farnham and trying to find him. Do you agree?"

Yael nodded, and Jack smiled, raised his fist and shouted (sotto voce), "Road Trip"! There was nothing more to do at the library, at least for now, so back to Jack's place we went, where his mother was preparing an enormous Friday night Shabbat dinner. His younger sister was home from the University of Toronto and his father was back from a business trip, so it was a full table and a lively one – everyone wanted to know everything about the quest, and our latest finds.

# Chapter XXXI

Saturday morning we took off in the family SUV, which was equipped with a GPS. That made navigation much easier on the back roads of Québec. It was about 75 kms, or just under an hour's drive, to Farnham. The weather was good, the roads were reasonable and we made good time. Farnham was officially Francophone, like the whole province, but in the last census close to 100 people had identified themselves as English Speakers, so hopefully we would be able to communicate with someone. This was really rural Québec, where the French spoken was closer to 15<sup>th</sup> century French rather than what is spoken in France today, and Jack's school French would have a hard time here.

At the Farnham town hall we struck gold. We went straight to the office of the tax collector, and asked if anyone knew of Fritz and Madeleine Schmitz. Once the clerk understood our question, he nodded, and pulled out a large ledger, where he looked them up. "*Ils habites le Rang de la Gare, a cote de Sainte Sabine*". It took a few attempts before we understood that this meant "They live on the Rang de la Gare, near Sainte Sabine".

The question now was – do we descend upon these poor, unsuspecting people, out of the blue and ask about their past and long forgotten relatives, or should we call ahead, or what? We debated the subject for a few minutes, and then decided "in for a penny, in for a pound". We found the house – really a farm house – easily (with the help of the GPS). With quite a bit of trepidation, the three of us walked up to the front door and rang the bell. After a minute, a woman about 50 years old opened it, and said: "*Oui?*"

Jack started to explain in his High School French that we were researching the history of the Canadian forces in WW II (which we had decided would be the starting point of our enquiries), when she held up her hand and said "You may speak in English, we are bi-lingual here in Farnham. Please come in and tell me how I can help you."

"Thank you Madame" we all said in unison. It was a relief that we would not have to translate constantly for all of us to understand what was going on.

I took the lead and asked her: "First of all, does M. Fritz Schmitz live here?"

She nodded "Oui", and waited. This was not going to be easy.

"Are you his daughter?" Again she nodded. "My name is Beatrice." Jack and I looked at each other with gleaming eyes. She was obviously named after his sister Beatrice, now Sister Beate.

"Do you know if he was a translator with the Canadian Forces in France during WWII?" Again the nod. "And before that, he was a translator with the German Occupying forces in France?" This time there was hesitation before she nodded.

"Would it be possible to speak with M. Schmitz himself?"

She thought for a moment and then replied: "Yes, I think so, but please remember that he is an old man of more than 80 years, and excitement is not healthy for anyone at his age. He speaks English quite well, so it will not be a problem for you. He's in the garden right now, I'll call him – please have a seat in the meantime."

The three of us sat on the edges of our chairs, in nervous anticipation. After a few minutes, Beatrice returned, and behind her came Fritz Schmitz. He walked straight up, with no indication of infirmity of age or anything like that, but slowly and determined. He sat down on a straight-backed chair opposite to us and said in quiet, correct English: "I understand that you would like to ask me some questions about my time in France."

I took the lead, and said "Yes, that is correct, but first of all I have some personal questions to ask you, if you don't mind, just to make sure about your identity."

"Please proceed, young man." Here I was the young man again! His German accent was still pronounced, despite having lived for almost 60 years in Francophone Québec.

"Your name is Fritz Schmitz?"

"Yes."

"You were a Prisoner of War in the Farnham POW Camp?"

"Yes."

"You were captured in the Falaise area of France in 1944?"

"Correct."

Now came the tough ones. "Before you were captured, was your name Fritz Georg Schmiltz, and not Schmitz?"

He visibly blanched, as if in fright, and he seemed to shrink into his chair.

I quickly said, in order to calm him down: "I'm sorry if this disturbs you M. Schmitz. Let me assure you that we are private citizens, doing private research, and that we have nothing to do with any government at all – not the Canadian, not the German, nor the French."

He seemed to relax a bit after that, and his daughter brought him a glass of water. I asked if I could continue, and he waved me on with his hand. "Now for the last difficult question. Are you the brother of Liesl Beatrix Schmiltz, and the son of Wilhelm Siegesmund Schmiltz and Ilse Margarete Steinpiltz?"

He looked at me like I was a magician or an emissary of the devil, and said: "Yes. How do you know this? No one knows this, not my daughter here, and not even my wife who passed away four years ago."

I took a deep breath, and started to explain. "First of all, you will probably be happy to know that at least as of two years ago, your sister was alive and very well, and I imagine that she still is. We will try to phone her in a while, after I have explained everything. We have a few more questions for you, but they are just to fill in some holes in our research. Are you willing to do this?"

He just nodded and said: "Beatrix is alive? I never knew that. How wonderful." He sat quietly and said nothing for a minute or two, gathering his thoughts, and then said: "Very well, please ask your questions and I will try to give you answers – and then can we call Beatrix?"

I assured him that we would, and let Jack tell the story of the quest, in a condensed version. When he came to the part about Normandy, and M. Daniel's story of the captured translator, he stopped and I asked: "Was that you? And if that was you, can you please fill in the story as to how you ended up here in Sainte Sabine?"

"Yes, that was me," he replied, and proceeded to tell the following tale.

As a translator for the Wehrmacht, he had taken part in many interrogations of French resistance fighters, from the *maquis*. He had seen what the fate of many of them had been – a firing squad or a hangman's noose – and had done all he could to help them avoid this end, by coaching them in how to answer and what to say. During one interrogation he had found out how to contact the local *maquis* group and had kept that information to himself. Two days later he had been sent to translate in a different location, and had gone there on a motorcycle. Near the location of the *maquis* group, he had dumped the motorcycle, and burned it, in the hope that the Germans would think he had been attacked by the *maquisards*. Having found the *maquis*, and having convinced them that he wished to join them and assist them, he was hidden away on a remote farm, in an underground cell, where he stayed until the Normandy invasion. During that time, he was used by the *maquis* to interrogate German soldiers they had captured, in order to find out about Wehrmacht movements and impending raids by the Gestapo.

During the battle of Falaise, the *maquis* group that he had been held by was nearly totally wiped out, and the remaining members decided they could no longer hold him safely, so they handed him over to the first allied unit they could find – the same North Nova Scotia Highlanders. After a swift interrogation to see who he was and why he was with the *maquis*, he was put to work again interrogating German prisoners. This time they were high-ranking officers, including Colonels and even Generals. On several occasions, the German prisoners had recognized him for what he was – a deserter from the Wehrmacht, and had threatened him with a violent end if they ever got out of captivity, or caught up with him any place else. There had apparently been hints of retribution even if and when Germany might loose the war – hints of an ODESSA type of organization were already in place then.

At the end of 1944, the Canadian Army had decided he was no longer needed, they had hundreds of translators by then, and had shipped him to the Farnham POW camp. He had been happy there, and enjoyed the relative freedom of the camp, to the extent that he even met one of the local girls and fell in love with her.

At the end of March, 1945, a new group of German POWs arrived at the Farnham camp, and he was horrified to see that one of the new arrivals was an SS *Oberst* (Colonel) by the name of Keitel, that he had helped to interrogate while working for the Canadian Army after the battle of Falaise. He had been a particularly nasty type, and had threatened Fritz on more than one occasion. When he arrived in Farnham, he was dressed in regular Wehrmacht uniform, not SS, and that made Fritz suspicious. He overheard a conversation where this *Oberst* was addressed by one of the camp guards as *Oberst* Frankl, which meant that he was hiding his true identity.

Fritz took the first opportunity to approach one of the camp commanders, Major John Templeton, and explained the situation, and begged him to get him out of the camp, before Keitel/Frankl recognized him and 'took care of him'. In return for exposing Keitel's true identity (which got him shipped back to Germany for trial as a war criminal), Fritz was given an early release from the camp and received immigrant status to stay in Canada. He married his girlfriend Madeleine, settled on the family farm, and never again thought about his past – until today.

When he was done, he sat back in his chair, and wiped his brow with his handkerchief, as the effort of telling this story had made him sweat. We could see that the fear of exposure from 60 years ago had not left him completely. Beatrice brought him a cup of tea from the kitchen, and after he had finished it, he looked at me and said quietly: "Could I speak with Beatrix now?"

"Certainly" I replied, "But you should know beforehand that after the war, she became a nun. She lived overseas for many years, but now is working at a hospice connected to the Oncology Department of the Göttingen Hospital."

Fritz just nodded, and I checked my watch to make sure we would not be waking Sister Beate when we called. Nuns get up early for morning mass, so it shouldn't be a problem. I took my cellphone and looked up the number I had for Sister Beate. Dialing Germany from Canada on an Israeli mobile phone was going to be horrendously expensive, but I didn't care. These two deserved to be reconnected, and after we were done here, they could write and call as they felt.

The connection was decent, and I reached Sister Beate easily. In my best German, I asked her first to sit down, as I had some exciting news for her. She said she was sitting, and then I told her in a minimum of words that we had found her brother Fritz, alive and well in Canada. There was an audible gasp from the other end of the line and then silence. After some ten or fifteen seconds, she ask quietly, "Are you 100% sure?"

I told her I was, and asked if she would like to speak with him, as he was sitting next to me. In her quiet voice she said, "Yes, please, and God Bless you young man." I passed the phone to Fritz and then the three of us went out into the garden, to give them some privacy – they deserved it after sixty years of separation.

Beatrice Schmitz joined us after a few minutes. "You know, I have never, ever heard my father speak German. It's quite strange. He never had any interest in anything German, he didn't read German books or newspapers. From the moment he was released from the POW camp here, he became a Francophone Canadian. I knew nothing about his time during the war, or in the camp here. It was just a fact – he had been a German soldier, he was captured by the Canadian forces and sent to the camp here in Farnham, and – *c'est tout*! In essence, his life began on the day he married my mother."

"Over the years, he learned English; he thought it was important to know both the Canadian national languages, and he has always thought of himself as a Canadian, not a Québécois. He was very thankful to Canada for letting him make a new life for himself here, and now I understood why."

Beatrice looked in through the front window and saw that her father had put the phone down. He was sitting in his chair, holding his face in his hands, and crying softly. I said to her: "I don't want to disturb him now, so could you just get my mobile phone for me and we'll be on our way." She nodded, went in, checked on her father and came back with the phone.

"Thank you for all you have done, it is really an amazing story."

"*De rien, mademoiselle.*" I said. On impulse I asked: "Do you own a computer with an internet connection?"

"Yes, of course. I work for the provincial government and need it for my job."

"Excellent. I will arrange for Sister Beate to have a computer, and have someone teach her how to use it if she doesn't know how already. You can then connect the two of them using Skype or some other video call program, and they can talk with each other whenever they want. It's the least we can do."

"You are very kind. Thank you again."

With that, we took our things and got into the car. Yael gave me a quick kiss and said: "You know you are really sweet, don't you?"

"*Moi?*"

"Yes, you. And on a totally different note – since everyone was so caught up in the moment in there, I had the sense of mind to turn on the mini-tape program on my laptop. I have the entire conversation recorded, so that we can refer back to it whenever we want or need to."

"You know you're quite clever, young lady. If you're not careful, I'll marry you."

"Whoops, too late. I'm already married!"

The ride back to Montreal was surprisingly quiet. It was strange to think that we were done – the quest was over, all the answers had been found. I think we all felt that way, and after parking the SUV in the family garage, we went down the street to a local pub, and had a drink. I raised my glass in a toast – "To *Onkel* Samuel, who took me on this journey, and to the two of you, who helped me reach the end. *L'Chaim!*"

But I was wrong.

# Chapter XXXII
## *The Last Piece of the Puzzle*

Yael and I were in no rush to get back to Israel, so we took advantage of being in Canada to have a real honeymoon – literally. We spent a leisurely month exploring the Canadian provinces of Québec and then Nova Scotia, which for me was an eye-opener. As an Israeli, I was overwhelmed by the enormous open spaces, and the seemingly unlimited quantities of water! But all good things must come to an end, and by the end of August we were back home in Jerusalem. I had classes to prepare, and the PhD thesis to write (and hopefully finish). Yael now had a job at a different, and more pleasant graphic studio not far from our apartment, and we were becoming settled and established.

When going through the accumulated material from my quest one day, I straightened out a pile of papers and felt something different in the middle. Upon further inspection, this turned out to be the "Monk's Manuscript" – the little piece of parchment that Mad Max had stolen from the Bodleian Library in Oxford, and had set him off on his insane journey that had led to my quest. It was fitting that I returned to this after the rest of the story was done, but I felt I needed to return it to the library, and perhaps learn from them what it was about.

Yael had never been to England, and neither had I, so we booked two seats on a British Airways flight for the next Saturday, reserved a room for two nights in a small Oxford Hotel, and I made some phone calls to the Bodleian. They had no idea that they were missing a manuscript, and would be pleased to get it back despite that. I made an appointment for the following Monday to meet their Keeper of Special Collections, and wrapped the manuscript carefully to make sure it would survive the journey

We spent the Sunday walking around Oxford, and taking a tour of the University. On Monday morning precisely at 11AM we knocked on the door of the Keeper's office. Prof. Arthur Christopher greeted us politely, and asked me to explain what I wanted to give him. I pulled out the cardboard case I had used to pack the manuscript, and handed it over to him. He put on a pair of white cotton gloves, so as not to transfer any skin oils to the parchment, and examined it under a large magnifying glass. After several minutes of looking at it from all sides, he put it down and said: "Well, first of all, thank you for giving this to us – or more correctly, returning it to us. Can you tell me how it came to be in your possession?"

"With pleasure" I replied, "but if you could first ask a linguist to have a look at it, I would really like to know what it says, and in the mean time I will tell you the story."

"Excellent idea." With that, he picked up his desk telephone and dialed a short number. "Could you please come to my office Charles?" he said.

A young man about my age came in. "This is Charles Wentworth, he is an expert on Medieval Manuscripts, he is the unofficial head of the Medieval French Manuscripts collection, and is fluent – if that is the correct term – in Medieval French.

We all shook hands in the most proper English fashion, and Prof. Christopher handed the manuscript to Charles Wentworth. "Could you please have a quick look at this, and come back when you have an idea what it says? Say in ten or fifteen minutes?"

The young expert just nodded his head, as he was already reading the parchment as he walked out of the room.

I gave the professor a quick, condensed version of the Quest, with details of how Mad Max had found the Monk's Manuscript and taken it back to Germany with him by mistake.

"What an extraordinary story," he said. "I'm sure that there is no record of this manuscript here in the Library, and I know of none that are missing under mysterious circumstances, so your mad professor seems to have been correct at least on that point. It probably came to us in some collection of manuscripts and had not yet been catalogued when he came across it."

I agreed with his conclusions. "The only thing we know about it is what Mad Max wrote is his diary. Keeping in mind that he was beyond a shadow of a doubt totally insane, and completely delusional, this is what he thought at least part of it said: "*... show the way from St. Michael to St. Michel*". He took this to mean that there was some underground, or under-water passage from Mount St. Michael in Cornwall, to the Monastery of Mont St. Michel in France. This was the basis of his entirely delusional project for winning the War for Germany and getting the Wehrmacht across the Channel and into England without anyone noticing."

Prof. Christopher shook his head in wonderment. "What a strange and evil man he must have been. I'm rather glad we won the war, and that it is you that is sitting here, and not him!" We all had a laugh over that and waited for Charles to return.

We chatted about research in general and the Quest in particular, and waited for Charles Wentworth to reappear. When he did, he was smiling. He put the manuscript fragment back on the desk, and also put a photocopy of another manuscript next to it. "What would you like to know?" he asked.

All three of us began throwing questions at him at once, and he raised his hands in mock fright. "One at a time, please."

"Sorry", I said. "This is the last piece of an enormous puzzle, and we are all very anxious to find out what it is all about."

"I understand. So ask away, just one at a time."

"Thanks. First and foremost, do you know anything about this manuscript fragment?"

"Yes, actually. If you look at the photocopy on the desk, you will see that your fragment fits a gap in another manuscript in our collection. The match is not perfect, there are small bits and pieces missing, but it is 100% clear to me that they are part of the same document."

"Wonderful!" I said. "Did our Mad Max actually steal this from your collection, despite what he wrote?"

"No, I think he is partially innocent, at least on this count."

"How so?"

"Our records show that we received the almost-complete fragment that is in the photocopy, sometime in early 1937. This would be just before your Mad Max arrived here to do research in the Library. His fragment – the Monk's Manuscript as you called it – does not appear in Library records, and I imagine that his assumption about what happened to it is more or less correct."

Jack held up one finger and said: "On the first count of the indictment – grand theft, the accused has been found innocent."

That got a chuckle from everyone. Jack continued: "Now, on the second count of bad translation – how do you find?"

Charles took the photocopy of his fragment and continued. "I won't read this out to you, you won't understand it and it isn't all that interesting. The short version is that this is NOT a religious text as your mad professor thought. It is a commercial document that deals with shipments from St. Michael's Mount in Cornwall to Mont St. Michel in Normandy. What he could not have known from his little bit, is that these shipments normally went from Cornwall first to Guernsey, in the Channel Isles. I've brought you a page from the Church of England web-site, which will help you understand."

> The ancient Priory Church of St. Michel du Valle, Guernsey, was built on a site associated with paganism. The exact date of the foundation of the church is unknown although it is not unreasonable to suppose that one was built here following the missionary endeavors of the Celtic Saint Sampson, who attempted to evangelize Guernsey in the middle of the sixth century. Around 968AD Monks from Mont St Michel in France founded a Priory and were granted land to maintain an income. The site, like that of Mont St Michel, formed an island at high tide, until Napoleonic times.

I read it quickly, and then gave it to Jack and Yael to read. "So if I understand you correctly, the St. Michel in the fragment has nothing to do with Mont. St. Michel in Normandy?"

"Correct!"

Jack held up two fingers, and said: "On the second count of jumping to conclusions with no facts to back him up, the verdict is Guilty."

"Correct. No researcher worthy of the name would have reached the conclusion he did, based on that one tiny fragment."

Yael broke in. "If everything you have said now is true, then what on earth is the fragment about?"

"Basically, the whole document together gives sailing directions for a ship or ships sailing from St. Michael's Mount in Cornwall, to St. Michel du Valle, Guernsey, and from there to Mont St. Michel in Normany. It also mentions several other stops along the way, at the Parish Church of Stoke Damerel, Devonport, and at St. Anne on Alderney in the Channel Isles.

Remember, sailing in those days was a primitive and risky business, and the ship would want to keep as close to shore as possible, before making the channel crossing."

He went on: "There is nothing mysterious about it, there are no secret passageways or tunnels or anything like that. It is a simple document, which between you and me, would not be worthy of any mention anywhere. We don't destroy such manuscripts even if they are not interesting, but no one would ever have looked at it again after it had been catalogued in 1937, except for you bringing us the missing piece."

I raised my hand, like I was back in school. "But what about that tunnel or stairwell or whatever it was that they were digging out on Mont St. Michel? It wasn't a secret passageway to England, but it is there. What could it have been?"

Prof. Christopher took up the challenge. "I cannot be sure, especially since I have not seen the site, but my guess is that it would lead to a portice in the walls that surround the Mont, where ships or barges could be loaded and unloaded. Either it was never completed, or at some time in history it was decided that it was no longer needed, so they walled it up."

We looked at each other and simultaneously shook our heads. Such a simple solution to such a convoluted and painful question.

Jack insisted on finishing the proceedings in style. "And on the third count, of attempting to sell a totally bogus, insane and ridiculous plan of action to Rudolph Hess, in the hope of being a hero to the German Nation, we find the nutcase Mad Max Vollendorf guilty of all the charges! And we can now lay this maniac to rest, for ever and ever."

We all breathed a sigh of relief – the Quest was finally over, all the parts were in place and there were no open questions. We could all go home again, get on with our lives – and write the story of *Onkel* Samuel from beginning to end.

# About the Author

Born in New York City of German-Jewish immigrant parents, Richard Steinitz studied at the State University of NY at Buffalo, and has been living in Israel since 1968. When not writing novels, he reads them in great quantities, and works for a multinational educational publisher. He and his wife Naomi are the parents of two grown children.

Though his own parents escaped the Holocaust, many relatives did not, and it has had an enduring effect on his life, and his writing.

Researching the background for his books is his favorite activity, and then comes reading mysteries!
*Kaplan's Quest* is his second novel.

Printed in Great Britain
by Amazon.co.uk, Ltd.,
Marston Gate.